State of Crisis

Zygmunt Bauman and Carlo Bordoni

polity

First published in 2014 by Polity Press

Polity Press
65 Bridge Street
Cambridge CB2 1UR, UK

Polity Press
350 Main Street
Malden, MA 02148, USA

ISBN-13: 978-0-7456-8094-1
ISBN-13: 978-0-7456-8095-8 (pb) ♥

A catalogue record for this book is available from the British Library.

Typeset in 11 on 13 pt Sabon
by Toppan Best-set Premedia Limited
Printed and bound in Great Britain by Clays Ltd, St Ives PLC

For further information on Polity, visit our website:
www.politybooks.com

State of Crisis

Contents

Preface

An essay written by four hands. Starting with the definition of 'crisis', this book develops along a path through the various forms taken on by the most serious problems of our changing times. It analyses current society according to Zygmunt Bauman in collaboration with Carlo Bordoni.

The basic thesis of this book is that the crisis facing the Western world is not temporary, but the sign of a profound change that involves the whole economic and social system and will have long-lasting effects. Bordoni theorizes a crisis of modernity and post-modernity, representing a contentious interregnum (a time-limited phenomenon that has left its aftermath in the present), while Bauman proposes new solutions within the framework of his theory of liquid society.

The final objective of this work is an original and previously unpublished analysis of the current condition of Western society, involving different aspects: from the crisis of the modern state to representative democracy, from neoliberal economics to the ongoing exit from mass society. A lively debate at a distance on the issues of the liquid society and an attempt to understand the present in order to prepare for the future. A sort of dictionary of the crisis, in which all the topics associated with it are discussed by the authors in an original way.

The authors are grateful to John Thompson for his encouragement and advice and wish to thank Elliott Karstadt, editorial assistant, Neil de Cort, production manager, and Leigh Mueller, copy-editor, for their professional help; moreover, Carlo Bordoni wants to thank Wendy Doherty for her careful help in translation of his text.

1

Crisis of the State

In the twenty-first century, what will replace the nation state (assuming it is replaced by something) as a model of popular government? We do not know.

Eric J. Hobsbawm[1]

A definition of crisis

Carlo Bordoni *Crisis*. From the Greek word κρίσις, 'judgement', 'result of a trial', 'turning point', 'selection', 'decision' (according to Thucydides), but also 'contention' or 'quarrel' (according to Plato), a standard, from which to derive *criterion*, 'means for judging', but also 'ability to discern', and *critical*, 'suitable to judge', 'crucial', 'decisive' as well as pertaining to the art of judgement.

A word that occurs frequently in newspapers, on television, in everyday conversation, which is used to justify, from time to time, financial difficulties, increases in prices, a decrease in demand, a lack of liquidity, the imposition of new taxes or all these things taken together.

Economic crisis is – according to dictionaries – a phase of recession characterized by a lack of investments, a decrease in production, an increase in unemployment, a term that has the general meaning of unfavourable circumstances, often linked to the economy.

Any adverse event, especially concerning the economic sector, is 'blamed on the crisis'. It is an attribution of responsibility absolutely depersonalized, which frees individuals from any involvement and refers to an abstract entity sounding vaguely sinister. This is because, some time ago, the word 'crisis' lost its original meaning and has since taken on a purely economic connotation. It has replaced other words that have been abused historically, such as 'conjuncture', which was often used in the 1960s and 1970s, when the general economic situation was more optimistic, and gave way to seasons in which mass consumerism reigned undisturbed.

Experiencing a period of 'conjuncture' was considered to be a painful but necessary transition in order to reach a new phase of prosperity. It was a time of adjustment in which to prepare the ground, refine strategies and recharge in order to regain strength and security and negotiate bargain deals as soon as things stabilized.

Conjuncture was a short period compared to all the rest. The term already implied a positive attitude that was confident about the immediate future, in contrast to other terms commonly used to indicate the economic difficulties in the past. After the Wall Street Crash of 1929, the *Great Depression* set in. Still today, this term, in comparison with 'conjuncture', evokes doomsday scenarios, and suggests a severe, long-term recession, combined with deep existential distress – something from which it is extremely difficult to recover, marked by the inevitable psychological implications.

The most serious crisis of modernity, that of 1929, which caused the stock-exchange collapse and gave rise to a chain of suicides, was skilfully resolved by applying the theories of Keynes: despite the deficit, the state invested in public works, employing labour at a time when there was no work to be found and companies were having to let people go; orders were stimulated and breathing space was given to industry, thus restarting the flywheel of the economy. However, the current crisis is different. The countries affected by the crisis are too far indebted and do not have the strength, perhaps not even the instruments, to invest. All they can do is make random cuts, which have the effect of exacerbating the recession rather than mitigating its impact on citizens.

Today we prefer to speak of 'crisis' rather than 'conjuncture' or 'depression'. It is certainly a more neutral term that has been used in many other contexts, apart from an economic one, and is therefore rather familiar. From matrimonial crises that upset the life of a married couple, to adolescent crises that mark the transition from puberty to adulthood, 'crisis' conveys the image of a moment of transition from a previous condition to a new one – a transition which is necessary to growth, as a prelude to an improvement in a different *status*, a decisive step forward. For this reason it strikes less fear.

As can be seen, 'crisis', in its proper sense, expresses something positive, creative and optimistic, because it involves a change, and may be a rebirth after a break-up. It indicates separation, certainly, but also choice, decisions and therefore the opportunity to express an opinion. In a broader context, it takes on the meaning of the maturation of a new experience, which leads to a turning point (on a personal level as much as on a historical–social level). In short, it is the predisposing factor to change that prepares for future adjustments on a new basis, which is by no means depressing, as the current economic impasse shows us.

Recently 'crisis' has become linked to the economic sector essentially to indicate a complex and contradictory condition, which cannot be defined as 'inflation', 'stagnation' or 'recession', but in which a series of causes and effects is combined in a jumble of conflicting issues.

In fact, this crisis is characterized by the simultaneous combination of an economic gamble on an international level (the causes) and the measures taken locally to deal with it (the effects). Both impact on the citizen in a different way, interacting and contributing to the complexity of a social malaise that is proving to be more and more important. The widespread perception is that the cure is worse than the disease, because it is more immediate and noticeable on the people's skin.

This crisis comes from afar. It has its roots in the 2000s, marked by the new outbreak of terrorism and the emblematic destruction of the Twin Towers in New York in 2001. It was no coincidence that the Twin Towers were part of the World Trade Center, the headquarters of the World Trade Organization. Premonition or coincidence? In fact, since then, despite the explosion of the 'new economy', the financial markets have begun to tremble, showing that globalization would not have led to anything good. The main concern for observers at the close of the twentieth century was, in fact, the consequences of the invasion of world markets by large multinational corporations – economic, but also cultural colonizations (challenged by the 'No logo' movement), which made us fear globalization as the triumph of a huge standardized and homogenized world-wide market, at the expense of small producers and commercial networks.

But the liberalization of borders, as well as having significant effects for personal liberty and communications, has also opened the way to a flood of economic difficulties. A stock market crash in Tokyo has immediate repercussions in London or Milan. So the speculative bubble on junk bonds, which started in South America and is responsible for the most serious collapse of the banking system ever, infiltrated Europe, triggering the present crisis, which we cannot see a way out of.

The current crisis is financial, while the crisis of 1929 was industrial: now the theories of Keynes could not be applied. Look at the case of Greece, where the huge contributions from the European Community only serve to reduce the deficit temporarily and fail to develop into new productive investments. The flywheel cannot restart.

Similarly, private companies have no interest in investing capital in the countries undergoing serious difficulties, partly because of the banking credit crunch, but especially because of inconsistent economic returns, a result of the reduction in consumption.

In this phase we witness the curious phenomenon of an increase in the price of essential goods, which goes against market trends (they should decrease as a consequence of the diminished demand): the rise in prices tries to compensate, in the short term, for the decrease in sales, remunerating the producer for losses suffered as a result of being unable to sell. At a later stage, if adequate corrective measures are not implemented, a fall in consumer prices slows production, bringing about a shortage of essential goods and causing new forced price increases that try to restore the balance between supply and demand. This situation triggers a wartime economy, with doubling of market prices (in the black market), that Europe tragically experienced in the last part of World War II.

When we move towards a severe recession, usually there is a general increase in the price of consumer goods (you only have to

do some shopping in a supermarket to notice it), along with the
stagnating or falling market value of real estate. It is the most
obvious sign of a serious failure, which, if not corrected, will
inevitably lead to an economic collapse. The decline in sales of
certain goods, such as real estate, alongside an increase in prices
of essential goods, immediately indicates a different destination
for the money supply which is used in consumption (rather than
being invested) or, if we are dealing with large amounts of capital,
is transferred abroad where it is safe and has a chance of regaining, at least in part, its lost profit.

The increase in consumer prices not only diverts resources from
investment and the real estate market, it also creates a sort of
'*Titanic* Syndrome', characterized by a contagious euphoria while
the country is sinking. A part of the population, which for the
moment has not yet been affected by the crisis, uses up its savings
and increases its spending (spending more than necessary, allowing themselves holidays, etc.), justifying their behaviour to themselves with the precariousness of existence: 'let's enjoy it while we
can' is their motto, as they carry on living as if nothing had
changed, closing their eyes to reality.

In others it can have that particular 'echo effect' that makes
them spend on the basis of the previous years' income, thus maintaining the same standard of living and then getting into debt. It
is a form of obvious psychological self-defence, in which individuals try to contain the anxiety that pervades them given the collapse
of all certainty for the future.

On the other hand, there are the cases of suicide. It is said there
have been over 1,200 cases of suicide in Greece alone because of
the economic crisis. There are those who drown while the privileged dance on the top deck of the ship, pretending not to see. Or
perhaps they are well aware of it but, for this very reason, they
stubbornly close their eyes to it.

Inflation is a different matter. The collapse of the value of
money, its progressive inconsistency in its relationship with consumer goods, have been avoided for the moment. Inflation is
linked with all the economic crises of modernity; it reached an
all-time record during the Weimar Republic (before Hitler's rise
to power in Germany), when the cost of a kilo of bread reached
1 million marks – or in Argentina in the 1970s, when the number
of pesos needed to pay for bread increased day by day in an

endless crescendo. Inflation is the worst consequence of any economic crisis, because it sweeps life savings away and reduces people to hunger in a very short time: money can no longer buy anything and despair sets in. A fast-acting cancer that propagates with the same speed of movement as the currency. The more quickly it changes hands, the less value it has. We are saved from inflation thanks to the euro. Greece will be saved from inflation, which should already be moving at galloping speed, as long as it remains within the euro zone. A return to the drachma would be fatal.

The euro is not an inflation-proof currency, but it is the currency of most of the states of the European Community and of the stronger states (starting with Germany) and they have no intention of falling into the Weimar trap a second time. They have the right instruments to keep it at bay and they impose them on everyone else. Among these instruments are, undoubtedly, a balanced budget, a cap on interest rates, a reduction in public debt and the consequent slowing-down of the circulation of money. This is called 'deflationary' politics (a far cry from the theories of Keynes, adopted to resolve the crisis of 1929) and, to our cost, we are paying the consequences.

Unfortunately, if this condition is not corrected by appropriate interventions, it in turn generates other problems in a disastrous chain reaction. Redundancies deprive families of purchasing power, burn up savings and lower consumption, which in turn is reflected in trade and production. It opens the way to stagnation, the most feared facet of the economic crisis, in which the state and the government, instead of reducing friction, push in the opposite direction and increase taxes, which only makes the situation worse.

A special feature of this crisis is its duration. The time of unfavourable 'conjunctures', which could be resolved over a short period, has come to an end. Now the crises – so vague and generalized because they involve much of the planet – take eons to turn around. They progress very slowly, in contrast to the speed with which all other human activities in contemporary reality actually move. Any forecast of a solution is continuously updated and then postponed until a later date. It never seems to end.

When one crisis ends, another, which in the meantime has come to lick round our borders, steps in to take its place. Or perhaps it is the same huge crisis that feeds on itself and changes over time, transforming and regenerating itself like a monstrous teratogenic entity. It devours and changes the fate of millions of people, making it the rule of life rather than the exception, becoming an everyday habit which we have to deal with rather than an occasional, annoying inconvenience to get rid of in the quickest way possible.

Living in a constant state of crisis is not pleasant, but it can have its positive side, since it keeps the senses vigilant and alert, and psychologically prepares us for the worst. We must learn to live with the crisis, just as we are resigned to living with so much endemic adversity imposed on us by the evolution of the times: pollution, noise, corruption and, above all, fear. The oldest feeling in the world that accompanies us through a reality marked by insecurity.

We will have to get used to living with the crisis. Because the crisis is here to stay.

Zygmunt Bauman   I get the impression that the idea of 'crisis' tends to drift nowadays back to its medical origins. It was coined to denote the moment in which the future of the patient was in the balance, and the doctor had to decide which way to go and what treatment to apply to help the ill into convalescence. Speaking of crisis of whatever nature, including the economic, we convey firstly the feeling of *uncertainty*, of our *ignorance* of the direction in which the affairs are about to turn – and secondly the urge to intervene: to *select* the right measures and *decide* to apply them promptly. When we diagnose a situation as 'critical', we mean just that: the conjunction of a diagnosis and a call for action. And let me add that there is an endemic contradiction involved: after all, the admission of the state of uncertainty/ignorance doesn't bode well for the chance of selecting 'right measures' and so prompting things to move in the desired direction.

But let me focus – as is, I gather, your intention – on the *economic* crisis. You start by reminding us of the horrors of the 1920s–1930s, against which each successive stumbling of the economy has since tended to be measured, and ask whether the current, post-credit-collapse crisis can be seen and described as a reiteration of that period, thereby throwing some light on its likely outcome. While admitting that there are numerous striking similarities between the two crises and their manifestations (first and foremost, massive and prospectless unemployment and soaring social inequality), I suggest that there is, however, one crucial difference between the two that sets them apart and renders comparing one to the other questionable to say the least.

While horrified by the sight of markets running wild and causing fortunes to evaporate together with workplaces, while forcing viable businesses into bankruptcy, victims of the late 1920s stock-exchange collapse had little doubt about where to look for rescue: to the state, of course – to a *strong* state, so strong as to be able to *force* the state of affairs to concur with its will. Opinions as to the best way out of the predicament might have differed, even considerably, but there was no disagreement about who might push the state of affairs onto the road eventually selected: of course the *state*, equipped with both resources indispensable for the job: *power* – that is, the ability to get things done – and *politics* – that is, the ability to decide which things ought to be done. You rightly mention Keynes in this context: along with the rest of the informed or intuitive opinion of the time, he put his wager on the resourcefulness of the state – his recommendations made sense in as far as the 'really existing' states could rise to meet popular expectations. And indeed, the aftermath of the collapse stretched to its limits the post-Westphalian model of a state armed with absolute and indivisible sovereignty over its territory and everything it contains, even in forms as various as the Soviet state-managed, German state-regulated and US state-stimulated economies.

This post-Westphalian model of the omnipotent territorial state (in most cases a nation-state) emerged from the war not only unscathed, but expanded, reinforced and reassured to match the comprehensive ambitions of a 'social state' – a state insuring all its citizens against the vagaries of fate, individual misfortunes and fear of indignity in any of the many forms (as fear of poverty, exclusion and negative discrimination, ill health, unemployment, homelessness, ignorance) that haunted the pre-war generations. The model of the 'social state' was also adopted, even if in a considerably cut-down rendition, by numerous new states and quasi-states emerging amidst the ruins of colonial empires. The 'glorious thirty' years that followed were marked by the rising expectation that all harrowing social problems were about to be resolved and left behind, and the haunting memories of poverty and mass unemployment would be buried once and for all.

In the 1970s, however, the progress ground to a halt, confronted with rising unemployment, seemingly unmanageable inflation, and the growing inability of states to deliver on their promise of comprehensive insurance. Gradually, yet ever more starkly, states manifested their inability to deliver on their promises; gradually, but apparently unstoppably, faith and trust in the potency of the state began to be eroded. Functions previously claimed and jealously guarded by the states as their monopoly, as well as being widely considered by the public and the most influential opinion-setters as their inalienable obligations and mission, seemed suddenly too onerous or too resource-greedy for the nation-states to carry. Peter Drucker famously declared that people need to, should and shortly will have to abandon hopes of salvation descending 'from above' – from the state or society – and the number of ears keen to absorb that message grew at an accelerating pace. In popular perception, aided and abetted by the chorus of a growing part of the learned and opinion-making public, the state was downgraded from the rank of the most powerful engine of universal well-being to that of a most obnoxious, perfidious and annoying obstacle to economic progress.

Was this another watershed, then, in the history of public mood? Was it another 'interregnum', or as the French would say 'rupture' – a stretch of under-defined and under-determined terrain as yet unvisited, unexplored and unmapped, which the old trusty vehicles seem unfit to negotiate, yet the new ones fit for the job still need to be designed, produced and put on the road? Yes, but, just as during the Great Depression of the 1920s–1930s, the opinion-setters, as well as gradually but steadily widening circles of the general public, claimed *to know* what kind of vehicles were called for to replace the old ones – once trusty yet increasingly rusty and overdue for the scrapyard. Once more, it seemed to be obvious what kind of a powerful force was destined, willing and able to lead the way out of the current crisis. This time, public trust was invested in the 'invisible hand of the market' – and indeed (as recommended by Milton Friedman, Ronald Reagan, Margaret Thatcher and the fast-expanding bevy of their enthusiastic subalterns, sycophants and acolytes – all busily digging up from disgrace and oblivion Adam Smith's pronouncements and recycling/

reshaping them for public use) in the magic power of bakers' greed, on which all those who wish freshly baked bread to appear daily on our breakfast table can rely. 'Deregulation', 'privatization', 'subsidiarization' were to accomplish what regularization, nationalization and communal state-guided undertakings so abominably and frustratingly failed to deliver. State functions had to be and were to be shifted sideways ('hived-off', 'out-sourced' and/or 'contracted out') to the market – that admittedly 'politics-free' zone – or dropped downwards, on the shoulders of human individuals, now expected to furnish individually, while inspired and set in motion by their greed, what they did not manage to produce collectively while inspired and moved by communal spirit.

After the 'glorious thirty' came the 'opulent thirty': the years of a consumerist orgy and all-but-continuous, seemingly unstoppable growth of GNP indices all over the place. The wager on human greed seemed to be paying off. Its profits came into view much earlier than its costs. It took a couple of dozen years to find out what fuelled the consumerist miracle: the discovery by the banks and the credit-card issuers of a vast virgin land open to exploitation – a land populated by millions of people indoctrinated by the precepts of a 'saving-book culture' and still in thrall to the puritan commandment to resist the temptation of spending unearned money. And it took yet a few years more to awaken to the sombre truth that the initially fabulous returns from investments in virgin lands must soon run out of steam, reach their natural limits and eventually stop arriving altogether. When that ultimately happened, the bubble burst, and the bright *fata morgana* of perpetually rising opulence vanished under a sky covered with dark clouds of prospectless redundancy, bankruptcies, infinite debt-repayment, drastic falls in living standards, shrinking life ambitions and, in all probability, of social degradation of the self-confident, upward-looking and boisterous classes to the status of a perplexed, defenceless and fear-stricken 'precariat'.

Was this another crisis of agency, then – another 'rupture' or interregnum? Yes, but with a difference – and a fateful, seminal one. As before, old vehicles of 'progress' are overdue for the scrapheap, but there is no promising invention in sight in which one could reinvest the hope of carrying all the rudderless victims out of trouble. After the loss of public trust in the wisdom and potency of the state, now it is the turn of the dexterity of the 'invisible hand of the market' to lose credibility. Every one of the old ways of doing things lies discredited, and the new ways are – at best – at the drawing board or experimentation stage. No one can swear, hand on heart, to the effectiveness of any. All too well aware of the hopes that failed, we have no potential runners-up to bet on. Crisis is a time for deciding what way of proceeding to take, but in the arsenal of human experience there seem to be no trustworthy strategies to pick from.

We are painfully aware, at least for a moment and until the human, all-too-human selective memory has done its job, that, if left to their own devices, the profit-guided markets lead to economic and social catastrophes. But should we – and, above all, could we – return to the once-deployed, yet now unemployed or under-employed, devices of state supervision, control, regulation and management? Whether we *should* is obviously a moot question. What is well-nigh certain, however, is that we *couldn't* – whatever answer we choose to the other question. We couldn't because the state is no longer what it used to be 100 years ago, or what it was then hoped it would soon become. In its present condition, the state lacks the means and resources to perform the tasks which effective supervision and control of the markets, not to mention their regulation and management, required.

Trust in the state's capacity to deliver rested on the supposition that both conditions of effective management of social realities – power and politics – are in the hands of the state, assumed to be a sovereign (exclusive and indivisible) master within its territorial boundaries: 'power' meaning the ability to get things seen through and done, and 'politics' meaning the ability to decide which things ought to be done and which things are to be sorted out on the global level – where much of the effective power to get things done already resides – and so to be avoided or undone. By now, however, the state has been expropriated of a large and growing part of its past genuine or imputed power (to get things done), which has been captured by the supra-state – global – forces operating in a politically uncontrolled 'space of flows' (Manuel Castells' term) – whereas the effective reach of the extant political agencies did not progress beyond the state boundaries. This means, purely and simply, that finances, investment capitals, labour markets and circulation of commodities are beyond the remit and reach of the only political agencies currently available to do the job of

supervision and regulation. It is the politics chronically afflicted
with the deficit of power (and so also of coercion) that faces the
challenge of powers emancipated from political control.

To cut a long story short: the present crisis differs from its historical precedents in as far as it is lived through in the situation
of a *divorce between power and politics*. That divorce results in
the *absence of agency* capable of doing what every 'crisis', by
definition, requires: choosing the way to proceed, and applying
the therapy called for by that choice. This absence, it seems, will
continue to paralyse the search for a viable solution until power
and politics, now in the state of divorce, are remarried. It also,
however, looks as though, under conditions of global interdependence, such remarriage is hardly conceivable inside one state,
however large and resourceful it might be. It looks like we are
now facing the awesome task of raising politics and its stakes to
an entirely new, and unprecedented, height.

A statism without a state

Carlo Bordoni   With regard to health, the word 'crisis' was used
in the past to indicate that the patient was in a serious condition
and faced dying. At that point, a consultation was called – that
is, a meeting of several medical specialists – to discuss which treatments should be administered. 'Consultation' is no longer used in
everyday language, especially after Dr House demystified physi-
cians' meetings, in which they talk about everything and try different treatments to see how the patient responds. Crisis has
suffered the same downgrading in other fields and 'is in crisis'; it
has moved to the field of psychology, referring to mood or the
existential, as well as the sentimental, condition.

Perhaps this is why the definition of 'crisis' is ill suited to the
current situation, which, at least in the economic sphere, seems to
be fairly stable. There is the risk of the term 'crisis' being used
deliberately to give the impression that the condition we are experiencing is only temporary and that we will soon be able to pull
out of it using the appropriate treatment.

The separation of power and politics is one of the decisive
reasons for the State's inability to make appropriate choices.
According to Étienne Balibar, the irreparable rift between local

and global has produced a kind of 'statism without a state' which takes place through a 'governance'.[2] This produces the paralysing effect you described of a *political system* (representative of the people, and therefore democratic) at a local level, reduced to the management of routine administration, unable to take on and solve the problems that *global power* (without political representation, and therefore fundamentally undemocratic) imposes with increasing frequency.

> Contemporary cities are a sort of big rubbish bin [Bauman's metaphor] into which global powers drop the problems they create for resolution. For example, mass migration is a global phenomenon caused by global forces. No mayor of any city in the world actually created the mass migration of people looking for bread, pure water for drinking and these sorts of conditions. People were set in motion by the impact of global forces, which deprive them of their means of existence and force them to move or die. So it's a vast problem. But they come to Milan, they come to Modena, they come to Rome, they come to Paris, they come to London and it is the mayor or the municipal council of the city who need(s) to deal with the issue. That's why I call it a rubbish bin. The problem comes from outside, but the problem has to be resolved, for better or worse, on the spot.[3]

Decisions are taken elsewhere by the powers that be, who, since they are supranational by their very nature, are not required to observe the local laws and ordinances: they are free from the limitations of political expediency as well as from needs of a social nature, in the name of objectivity and a principle of equity that does not express real justice.

The separation between the two levels, between the global and the local, between power and politics, would have remained unresolved and conflicting if power had not tried to 'interfere' in politics – to recuperate the difference, the distance between the two terms, and try to standardize their behaviour. It does so in the only way possible, by taking the place of *tout court* politics in the management of the local/national and, where this is not possible, by making the appropriate political decisions with consistent persuasion and/or subordination. With control over politics, the global power can now eagerly dominate society and prevent any resistance.

Balibar focuses on a form of 'governance' that has replaced the direct, tangible relationship between the state and the citizen: 'The European Union . . . is only the ghost of a state, because it does not have any really effective element of collective identification . . . A similar structure anticipates perhaps the form of survival of the state institution of citizenship, which is in our future and which would actually represent, under the name of governance, a form of *statism without a state.*'[4]

'Governance' is replaced by the state in relation to politics. The inconsistency of national governments, their inability to adapt to change and to meet the new organizational requirements and provide the safety net that the process of globalization requires, means that the need for community participation, the *sine qua non* condition for every kind of civil society, looks for satisfactory answers elsewhere. Answers that are not always fit for purpose, but can be driven by emotion, resentment, fear, or even by that *voluptas dolendi* that Étienne de la Boétie called 'voluntary servitude' (a sycophantic acquiescence and submission to any form of power). In any case, they question every current form of democracy or, at best, create the conditions for new, previously unknown, forms of democratic representation.

Inconsistent answers – because they do not resolve the problem in all its complexity – mainly take the form of an anti-politics, a kind of rejection and nausea in the face of a relationship now worn thin. Anti-politics is an inaccurate term: formally it indicates an aversion of the citizenry (there is no mention of the people, because it presupposes a reciprocal link with the sovereign state) to policy itself. Rather than anti-politics, one could speak of 'anti-partyism', but it is clear to everyone that the use of this term is fairly ambiguous and conforms to the system, sending a negative and accusatory message to those who practise 'anti-politics'.

But anti-politics – as recognized by Balibar – gives rise to populism and nationalism, both dangerous and subject to the most devastating deviations. It often proves to be the prelude to tyrannical and authoritarian regimes, as demonstrated by recent history. It starts from the rejection of politics ('politics is a dirty thing') and, through the exaltation of charismatic figures, able to attract the attention and fondness of the masses, it manages to justify the dictatorship of the strong man, the only one who can take on the daunting task of putting things right. There is always a man of providence ready to intervene when the relationship between the state and citizens has deteriorated.

Nationalism is anachronistic and short-sighted. Going back to traditional values, tightening the ranks and valuing only what is known locally and territorially delimited, seems today to be a futile effort – especially if we think it is possible to give back the absolute power of decision-making and policy management to a local area that has to deal with the global economy. Like a certain kind of populism, nationalism today does not go beyond the drama of a tragicomic operetta, exaggerated by the media for the entertainment of the masses, who are quite rightly worried.

But the most disturbing thing is the 'statism without a state', towards which we launched ourselves with naive indifference. 'Governance' has taken the place of a functional government, bound by a relationship of trust with the public. Hidden behind a mass of increasingly chaotic and impenetrable bureaucracy, 'governance' manages the community that has lost its state guardian due to an inconsistent delegation that gave rise to the idea of 'false democracy', because it lacks both the conditions that make the 'proxy' democratic: political direction and control. In fact, no one stipulates the orientation of community policy and its priorities (there is no programme with which to make a comparison); nobody checks the work of the community and its adherence to the will and intentions of the people. Faced with this grave double lacuna, it is not possible to talk about democracy, while it undermines even the threatened separation of politics and power. The two terms appear so far apart as to be fragmented, controversial and interfering.

If power is managed by the markets, by financial groups, by supranational forces that evade any democratic control, then politics is a controversial and frayed subject. It takes on many faces: there is the policy of the European community, conditioned by the stronger states and markets (who are able to address 'their' policy through *lobbies*); the policy of the nation-states that has no power, but is perfectly self-referential and self-perpetuating; a local policy that has limited and reduced power simply to manage the existing situation, with no chance of intervening in the impenetrability of 'governance'. In addition to a wide range of policies with no power and power with no policies that are used in organizations, institutions and services with conflicting autonomy.

This is not an adaptation to the conditions of crisis or an ideological choice, but a change in the nature of 'politics'. A real form
of 'anti-politics' that neutralizes dissent, that eliminates any real
antagonism as a precautionary measure, reduces the political
parties to competing with each other over illusory problems that
are designed to divert public attention from the real problems.

Anti-politics ensures the continuation of the political game
going on between the parties, but deprives it of social significance,
since the citizen is obliged to look after his own well-being: the
'state directs and controls its subjects without being responsible
for them',[5] implementing a sort of neoliberal 'governance', which
turns out to be a technique of indirect, but not ineffective,
government.

This form of autonomy of the parties responds to neoliberal
ideology which clearly originates in the United States, where it has
a long tradition and is fully functional in the process of demassification. In mass society, the need for tight social control forced
a bond between the state and the citizen through the administration of services and the direct management of activities that, on
the one hand, provided security, and on the other formed a strong
bond of dependence on which one could sit back and be wafted
along.

If mass society is the latest stage of modernity, its best attempt
to maintain social control in the face of increasingly threatening
divergent forces that call hegemony into doubt, it is clear that
from the moment the process of demassification in postmodernity
begins, the individual is increasingly left to his own devices.

The ties between the state and the citizen are weakened, society
loses cohesion and becomes 'liquid'. In the words of Eric J.
Hobsbawm in the epigraph above, there is talk of the end of the
state and its constitutive mode.[6] Demassification is indeed a process
of awareness of the autonomy of the individual, but also a state
of isolation and solitude for the global citizen, of loss of the social
ties that the mass somehow assured.

The frenetic drop in consumption is an important signal. The
'glorious thirty years' (between 1940 and 1970) and 'opulent
thirty years' (between 1970 and the end of the century) experienced a period of consumer enthusiasm and irresponsible optimism, which had a profound effect on the lifestyle, culture
and behaviour of the individual (we just have to think of the

ephemeral splendour of the 'new economy', the emergence of the 'preppy' style, the expansion of the movable goods and real estate market).

The 'glorious thirties' and 'opulent thirties' were the result of a rapid evolution of the welfare state and unlimited confidence in its ability to ensure the welfare and security of everyone, but also of a precise political strategy (when politics still held power) that had replaced the totalitarianism of violent repression and intrusion into the private lives of citizens with the 'totalitarianism of consumption,' a novel way to secure social control with less aggressive, but no less effective, methods.

Unlike classical liberalism, which looked at a purely market model, left to private enterprise and free competition, without any state intervention ('more market, less state'), neoliberalism nests within the state itself. Wendy Brown argues that neoliberalism, in contrast to classical liberalism, tends to empower citizens to make entrepreneurs of themselves and therefore to establish an unprecedented ethic of 'economic calculation', which applies to public benefit activities that the government used to guarantee.[7]

The practice of neoliberalism subjects the social functions of the state to economic calculation: an unusual practice, which introduced the viability criteria into public services, as if they were private companies, regulating the fields of education, health, social security, employment, scientific research, public service and safety under an economic profile.

Neoliberalism, therefore, removes the responsibility of the state, makes it relinquish its traditional prerogatives and moves towards their gradual privatization.

The loss of power results in a weakening of economic policy, which in turn is reflected in social services. The crisis of the state is due to the presence of these two elements: the inability to make concrete decisions on an economic level and, consequently, the inability to provide adequate social services.

A result of this is fiscal tightening, resorting to *deregulation*, *devolution* of institutional prerogatives, which are increasingly delegated to individuals: all of this with the objective of ensuring the existence and maintenance of the state apparatus and its privileges, which have become fewer and fewer. At this stage, the state in crisis, rather than being provider and guarantor of public welfare, becomes 'a parasite' on the population, concerned only for its own survival, demanding more and more and giving less and less in exchange.

The political choices made today, in the absence of real power to 'make things right', appear only as a stopgap for the protection of the privileges acquired: an extreme form of self-defence which conjures the image of being locked up in a well-armoured bunker and equipped with every comfort, while Berlin is burning.

Zygmunt Bauman   Let me start from the point at which you stopped. I have an impression that no 'choices', or indeed 'decisions' are currently made by state governments except when they are forced to make them (or at least pretend that they make them) by other, more resourceful governments of more resourceful countries, or by amorphous and anonymous forces unrecorded in any State's constitution and called variously 'realities of the day', 'world markets', 'investors' decisions' or just 'TINA' ('There Is No Alternative').

Indecision, prevarication and procrastination are today the names of the game (even when, as all too often, it involves the 'classified' stuff). What governments are, at most, capable of, are what I call 'settlements' – interim agreements that from the start are not convincing and not meant to last, at best are hoped/prayed to survive till the next European Council gathering, or indeed to the next opening of the stock exchanges. Note how often the resolutions announced today are proclaimed (in a bizarre reversal of the usual sequence of causes and effects, or decisions and their consequences), legislated to become 'valid' and put into operation several years later – thereby giving them an option of being forgotten in the meantime or overtaken by events no one can predict – and so of becoming retrospectively stillborn.

And there are good reasons for indecision taking over, in the company of its brothers-in-disarmament, the offices once occupied – but now vacated – by planners, strategists, designers, commanders and other varieties of decision-making addicts. One of the most seminal of these reasons is the 'double bind' in which governments of the day invariably find themselves in democratic countries. All of them are exposed to two contradictory pressures whose demands, more often than not, are impossible to reconcile. Two pressures mean that the governments are obliged to look simultaneously in two opposite directions, reckoning with both though having little hope of earning the approval of either of them for their own middle-path, inescapably wishy-washy resolutions. Given the distance separating the sites from which the two pressures emanate, looking both ways is much more likely to result in a squint than in an acceptable compromise. A double bind has an effect not dissimilar from that of a straitjacket. Surely the outcome, if not the intention, is in both cases identical: incapacitation – severe limitation of moves, particularly the moves undertaken by the object of binding on its own initiative, for a purpose of its own choice.

The two pressures in question come, respectively, from the electors who are capable of putting the government out of, as much as in, office – and forces that are already globalized, free to float with little if any restriction in the politics-free extraterritorial 'space of flows' and able to avail themselves of the advantages of such freedom to frustrate, and ultimately make null and void, any decision taken by any government of a territorial state if it finds it contrary, or even insufficiently conforming, to its interests. Unlike the elected rulers themselves, forces holding them in that second bond of the 'double bind' owe no loyalty to electors and are neither obliged to listen to their grievances nor in the frame of mind to sacrifice their own interests for the sake of silencing them.

One of the defining traits of 'democracy' is the holding of periodical elections of the people at the helm. On condition that the results of the elections are not forged or obtained through coercion or its threat, those people are believed to represent the citizens' interests – or at least what they asserted to be in their interest at the time of polling. Any political party and any politician standing for election must therefore listen attentively to the people's voices in order to check their own platforms against what the electors are willing to support. They must phrase their published programmes and compose their electoral speeches in a way they hope will be relevant to the grudges and postulates of the electors. They must promise to be attentive to their grudges and seriously consider the implementation of their postulates. This is, however, easier said than done – at least done convincingly: pre-election promises are after all known to be, well-nigh routinely, swept under the office carpets shortly after the victory celebration. The wise-after-the-fact electorate is likely to remember that experience and politicians may need to make promises nevertheless – however great the risk of being voted out of office three or four years later might be.

The idea of territorial boundaries of sovereignty presumed by the Westphalian formula, together with the later added codicil of the natural and/or divinely blessed union of nation and state, have subsequently been exported by European *conquistadores* to the rest of the world, and were deployed in the period of European colonialism and applied in the overseas outposts of the emerging and burgeoning Europe-centred empires as much as they had been practised originally in their European metropolises. As a lasting trace of the European colonialist adventure, the Westphalian formula – mainly in its secularized, yet in some cases also in its original, form – remains in our postcolonial era, in theory if not in actual practice, the inviolable, universally binding and seldom – if ever – explicitly contested, organizing principle for human cohabitation on Earth.

The snag is that it is also counterfactual, and increasingly so – its premises being delusionary, its postulates unrealistic and its pragmatic recommendations ever less plausible. In the course of the last half-century, the processes of deregulation originated, promoted and supervised by state governments voluntarily joining or pushed into joining the so-called 'neoliberal revolution', have resulted in the growing separation and rising probability of divorce between power (that is, the capacity to get things done) and politics (that is, the ability to decide which things need and ought to be done). For all practical intents and purposes, much of the power previously contained inside the borders of the nation-state evaporated and flew into the no-man's land of the 'space of flows', whereas politics has remained as before territorially fixed and constrained. The compact of power and politics, the *sine qua non* condition of effective action and purposeful change, has in effect been split into a power freed from all but rudimentary political control, and politics suffering a permanent and growing deficit of power. That process acquired all the markings of a self-propelling and self-intensifying tendency. Seriously drained of powers and continuing to weaken, state governments are compelled to cede, one by one, the functions once considered a natural and inalienable monopoly of the political organs of the state into the care of already 'deregulated' market forces, evicting them thereby from the realm of political responsibility and supervision; and as for the task of tackling the adverse and potentially socially destructive effects of the endemic market tendency to an unbridled pursuit of profit at the expense of all other values, it has been 'subsidiarized' to what Anthony Giddens called the 'realm of life politics' – a realm left to the initiative, ingenuity, stamina and chronically inadequate resources of the individual.

The two parallel processes of 'contracting out' some state functions to market forces while 'subsidiarizing' quite a few others to 'life politics' in turn result, however, in the decline in popular trust in governments' ability to deal effectively with the multiple threats to the existential condition of their citizens. It is not that one political party or another is seen as having failed the test; the evidence accumulates that a change of guard prompts only minimal, if any, changes in governmental policies – and even less in the volume of hardships associated with the struggle for survival under conditions of acute uncertainty. It is the system of representative democracy itself – designed, elaborated and put in place by the builders of the modern nation-state – whose popular credentials are crumbling. Citizens believe less and less that governments are capable of delivering on their promises.

They are not wrong. One of the tacit yet crucial assumptions underlying trust in the efficacy of parliamentary democracy is that what the citizens decide in elections is who will rule the country for the next few years and whose policies the elected government will attempt to implement. The recent collapse of the credit-grounded economy brought the bankruptcy of that arrangement into spectacular relief. As John Gray, one of the most insightful analysts of the roots of the present-day world-wide instability, observes in the preface to the new (2009) edition of his *False Dawn: The Delusions of Global Capitalism* when asking why the recent economic collapse failed to increase international cooperation and instead released centrifugal pressures: 'governments are among the casualties of the crisis, and the logic of each of them acting to protect its citizens is greater insecurity of all'.[8] And this is because 'the worst threats to humankind are global in nature', while 'there is no prospect of any effective global governance to deal with them'.

Indeed, our problems are globally produced, whereas the instruments of political action bequeathed by builders of nation-states were reduced to the scale of services *territorial* nation-states required; they prove therefore singularly unfit when it comes to handling global, *extraterritorial* challenges. For us, continuing to live in the shadow of the Westphalian settlement, they are, all the same, the only instruments we can thus far think of and are inclined to turn to in moments of crisis, despite their jarring insufficiency to secure a territorial sovereignty, the *sine qua non* condition of that settlement's practical viability. The widely observed and predictable result is the frustration caused and bound to be beefed up by the inadequacy of means for ends.

To put it in a nutshell: our present crisis is first and foremost a *crisis of agency* – though ultimately it is a *crisis of territorial sovereignty*. Each formally sovereign territorial unit might serve nowadays as a dumping ground for problems originating far beyond the reach of its instruments of political control – and there is pretty little it can do to stop this, let alone pre-empt it, considering the amount of power left at its disposal. Some formally sovereign units – indeed a growing number of them – have been demoted in practice to the rank of local police precincts struggling to secure a modicum of law and order necessary for the traffic whose comings and goings they neither intend, nor are able to control. No matter how great the distance between sovereignty *de jure* and their sovereignty *de facto*, all of them however are bound to seek *local* solutions to *globally* generated problems – a task far transcending the capacity of all except a handful of the richest and most resourceful among them.

Once caught in a double bind, governments are left with little choice but to pray that before the date of the next election is announced, their loyal, obedient service to the 'second bond forces' will be repaid with a rising heap of investment and trade contracts – and so also, most importantly, with the 'feel-good factor', by common agreement the chief advisor of the people in the polling booth. Let's note, however, that signals are getting thicker on the ground of this kind of calculation no longer working as expected. It is not just that the elected politicians fail to deliver on their promises; nor do the 'second bond forces' (stock exchanges, itinerant capitals, venture bankers and their like, summarily called 'world investors' in the current politically correct language) deliver according to the politicians' expectations. There is nothing therefore, not even a glimmer of light at the end of the tunnel, with which to compensate the frustration of the electorate and assuage their wrath. Citizens' mistrust and resentment spread to the whole of the political spectrum except perhaps its thus far (but for how long?) marginal, ephemeral and eccentric parts, publicly demanding an end to the failed and discredited democratic regime. Choices made in the polling booth are now seldom motivated by trust invested in an alternative; more and more often, they are results of another frustration caused by the botched job done by the incumbents. Parties able to boast a record of holding onto office for more than one term become ever fewer and farther between.

Now that the nation-state institutions are no longer competent players promising to blaze more passable trails and repair more harrowing blunders, what force, if any, can possibly fill the vacant position/role of the agent of societal change? This is a moot question, and an increasingly contentious one. There is no shortage of exploratory sallies. There are plenty of attempts to find new instruments of collective action, that fit better in the increasingly globalized setting than the political tools invented and put in place in the post-Westphalian era of nation-building – instruments that, for that reason, stand more chance of bringing popular will to fruition than ostensibly 'sovereign' state organs, squeezed in a double bind, can hope to regain. Such reconnaissance sorties keep coming from many quarters of society and particularly from the 'precariat', a rapidly growing stratum soaking up and absorbing whatever remained of the former industrial proletariat alongside ever-wider chunks of the middle classes. That stratum is so far 'united' solely by the sensation of life lived on quicksand or at the foot of a volcano. What renders the prospects of the reconnaissance units being consolidated into a serious – weighty and durable – political force rather dim, is that there is little in the social condition and interests of their participants that could be hoped to keep them together and inspire them to work together long enough to be recycled into trustworthy, reliable and effective tools fit to replace those whose inadequacy to the present tasks and ever more evident indolence triggered the present experiments in the first place. One of these ongoing experiments, figuring most prominently in the output of public media, is a phenomenon collated under the label of the 'movement of the indignant', drawing on mushrooming yet variegated experiences from Tahrir Square to

Taksim Square via Zuccotti Park. Harald Welzer[9] may be on the right track when he seeks the deep causes of that phenomenon in a growing public realization that 'individualist strategies have a mainly sedative function. The level of international politics offers the prospect of change only in a distant future, and so cultural action is left with the *middle* level, the level of one's own society, and the democratic issue of how people want to live in the future' – even if in many, perhaps most, cases, that knowledge is rather subliminal or poorly articulated.

Were Marx and Engels, those two hot-headed and short-tempered youngsters from Rhineland, setting down today to pen their almost two-centuries-old *Manifesto*, they could well have started it from an altered observation: that 'a spectre hovers over the planet; the spectre of indignation. . .'. Reasons to be indignant are, indeed, aplenty – one can, however, surmise that a common denominator of otherwise fairly varied original triggers and the yet more numerous inflows they attract as they gather publicity is the humiliating, self-esteem-and-dignity-defying-and-denying pre-monition of ignorance (no inkling of what is going to happen) and impotence (no way of preventing it from happening). The old, allegedly patented ways of tackling life-challenges don't work anymore, while new and effective ones are nowhere in sight or in abominably short supply.

One way or the other, indignation is there, and we have been shown a way of unloading it, albeit temporarily: through going to the streets and occupying them. The recruiting pool for poten-tial occupiers is enormous, and growing day by day. Now that they have lost faith in a salvation coming from 'on high' as we know it (that is, from parliaments and governmental offices) and are looking for alternative ways of getting the right things done, people are taking to the streets in a voyage of discovery and bouts of experimentation. They transform city squares into open-air laboratories, in which tools of political action they hope will match the enormity of the challenge are designed or come across by chance, put to the test, perhaps even pass a baptism of fire.

It is these kinds of problems that the European Union is hoped/expected/required to deal with and eventually to solve. The prob-lems in question have a common denominator: a crisis of agency, of trust in the extant agencies, and increasingly of popular trust in the virtues of democracy and its attractiveness. The European Union is one of the currently most advanced attempts to find, or design from scratch, a local solution to globally produced problems.

Europe, just like the rest of the planet, is nowadays a dumping ground for globally generated problems and challenges. But, unlike that rest of the planet and almost uniquely, the European Union is also a laboratory in which the ways to confront those challenges and tackle those problems are designed, debated and tested in practice on a daily basis. I would go as far as suggesting that this is one (perhaps even the sole) factor that makes Europe, its dowry and contribution to world affairs, exclusively significant for the future of the planet, which is faced with the prospect of a second seminal transformation in the modern history of human cohabitation – that of the crushingly toilsome leap, this time, from the 'imagined totalities' of nation-states to the 'imagined totality' of humankind. In that process, still in its initial and precocious stage yet one that has to proceed if the planet and its inhabitants are to survive, the European Union stands a chance of performing the combined/blended tasks of making a reconnaissance sally, setting up a way-station and creating a frontier outpost. These are not easy tasks, and anything but guaranteed to succeed – as well as bound to confront most Europeans, *hoi polloi* and their elected leaders alike, with a lot of friction between conflicting priorities and hard choices. But, as the French president François Hollande put it in his speech on 14 July 2013: 'Politics is not magic, not a bag of tricks, but a matter of will, strategy and coherence.' It is indeed. And so is the future of European unification – and, through it, of Kant's two-centuries-old dream of the *allgemeine Vereinigung der Menschheit*.

J. M. Coetzee, one of the greatest living philosophers among the writers of novels, and one of the most accomplished living novelists among philosophers, noted in his *Diary of a Bad Year* that 'the question of why life must be likened to a race, or of why the national economies must race against one another rather than going for a comradely jog together, for the sake of the health, is not raised'.[10] And he adds: 'But surely God did not make the market – God or the Spirit of History. And if we human beings made it, can we not unmake it and remake it in a kindlier form? Why does the world have to be a kill-or-be-killed gladiatorial amphitheatre rather than, say, a busily cooperative beehive or anthill?'[11] These are simple words, simple questions, no less weighty and convincing for the absence of a sophisticated argument spiked with academic jargon and concerned more with taking a leaf from the spirit of markets and scoring a point than with appealing to good sense and spurring human reason out of its slumber and into action. Indeed, why? Coetzee's question needs to be borne in mind whenever we try to comprehend the present predicament of the European Union: whenever we try to find out how we've found ourselves in it and what, if any, are the exits that are not yet locked forever. Present-day necessities are but sedimented and petrified leftovers from yesterday's choices – just as present-day choices beget the self-evident 'facts of the matter' in the emergent realities of tomorrow.

State and nation

Carlo Bordoni   Before we delve into the reasons for the crisis of the state let me clarify the meaning of 'nation'. 'Nation' has a cultural connotation and its distant origins are historically much older than those of the state: it is still recognizable as a nation even when its borders have not been marked out and, at least formally, it is still not a state with its own laws. A population that is recognized as a nation feels free in the territory in which it lives and does not need to set limits on freedom of movement within the space that it feels belongs to it.

And yet a country can continue to exist only if it exists as a state that reinforces its identity and ensures precise territorial limits, because, while the idea of 'nation' is a feeling, the state – more pragmatically – needs a territory in which to take root. According to Jürgen Habermas, on the other hand, national community does not precede the political community, but is the product of it.[12] A statement we partially accept, if we admit that the idea of nationality can mature only within a state (as Massimo D'Azeglio declared, 'Unfortunately, Italy has been made, but the Italians will not be'), which, however, does not take into account the need for the presence of a core of national feeling (although one not yet institutionalized) on which to build a state.

State and nation go together and support each other, but something began to change in the late 1970s and subsequent decades, corresponding to the dissolution of modernity.

The anthropologist Arjun Appadurai was the first to report that the concept of nation was entering a crisis, because it was cultural identity itself that was first damaged by the change taking place.[13] What was called into doubt was the idea of the national community, based on the same language, same customs, same religion, same culture.

The opening of borders is preceded by a cultural openness that upsets the age-old certainties. The idea of nation endures while linguistic, religious or political minorities are 'confined' temporarily or geographically in 'enclaves' in ghettos, in refugee camps or in shelters. Then, when the diasporic communities begin to see recognition of their rights as citizens with full entitlements, and then demand recognition of their 'diversity' with respect to the obligation to integrate (the customary path towards equality), the 'unity' of the nation begins to crumble.

Already in the 1990s, Appadurai was talking about postnational states, in which diasporic communities were no longer occasional or temporary occurrences, but long-lasting ones built into the system, an integral part of the culture and history of the country. The term 'postnational' better defines the earlier concepts of 'multinational' and 'international', which remain fairly strongly related to economic, legal and practical dependence with the state of reference, until the entire system is weakened.

We live in a constant state of crisis, and this crisis also involves the modern state, whose structure, functionality, effectiveness (including the system of democratic representation) are no longer suited to the times in which we live.

There are many critical issues facing the modern state and the causes are numerous: some induced by profound historical and cultural changes that took place during the final years of the twentieth century and the first decade of the third millennium, others by political and economic choices that led to grave consequences in people's daily lives, further exacerbating their distance from the institutions.

In the first place, there was the demise of the post-Westphalian model. This appears crucial to an understanding of the present condition which started with the loss of meaning of this model of balance between States, which has stood for centuries and has been the cornerstone of international relations. The Treaties of Westphalia (Münster and Osnabrück) in 1648 (then essentially reconfirmed by the statute of the United Nations) established some basic principles on which to base the rights and limits of the modern state, the new civil system that was born from the ashes of feudalism and that Hobbes represented metaphorically in Leviathan: a form of monstrous strength made up of all the men who gathered together and recognized each other in a superior unity.

Based on the principle of limited sovereignty, the post-Westphalian model recognizes in the modern state absolute and indivisible sovereignty over its territory and ownership in international relations, of which it is the sole subject.

If, for a long time, state and nation have been able to live together, united on a historical and legal level by the insolubility of the fundamental principles that modernity assured, it was thanks to the agreements made in the Treaties of Westphalia, at the end of the long religious war that had shattered Europe for thirty years. Since then, modern states, in the form that we have known for centuries, have standardized the so-called 'post-Westphalian model', which sets down the rules for universal stability and recognizes the full sovereignty of a state within its own borders.

In the third millennium, it is the post-Westphalian model itself that enters into crisis, dragging with it the modern state, whose own crisis is triggered not only by the opening of borders, but also by the inability demonstrated in maintaining its commitments to its citizens. In this phase, it is the 'internal' boundaries that create problems. Security, defence of privilege, identity, recognition and cultural traditions, which once coincided with the boundaries of the post-Westphalian state, are now altered, uncertain, liquid. They are no longer reliable.

The dissolution of geographical or temporal limits imposed on diasporic communities leads to the well-known phenomenon of the turnaround: if, in the past, it was the majorities that enclosed the minorities in 'enclaves', now it is the same majorities that shut themselves inside the 'gated communities', protected by private security guards, by electronic controls and security systems – jealous of the privacy that is no longer guaranteed on the outside.

Now it is clear how this model entered into crisis with the development of globalization, whose explosive force has erased the boundaries between states and undermined any claim of absolute sovereignty. But the consequences of globalization are not limited only to undermining the rules of international relations; they have also led to a further upheaval, removing the power of the nation-states and raising it to a higher level. Now it is distant and spread on a global plane, and separated from politics, with which, up to now, it had been intimately linked. Hobbes' Leviathan, deprived of its operating arm, is reduced to a mutilated body that wallows in its impotence. It gets agitated, argues and proclaims, but cannot do anything even when it has made momentous decisions, because the operational side is the responsibility of others. This one no longer belongs to it.

The separation of politics and power is lethal for the modern state – especially if it is a democratic state, whose constitution has promised its citizens to let them take part in common decisions that now are taken by bodies that are non-democratically appointed and not controlled from beneath. The tragedy of the modern state lies in its inability to implement at a global level the decisions taken locally. The citizens, for example, elect their representatives to the European Parliament, who, in turn, elect committees and subcommittees, where executive decisions are taken by the ultimate organizational bodies, formed on the basis of a series of institutional changes, the complexity of which should be a guarantee of impartiality and independence.

If it were just a matter of bureaucracy, complicated by the presence of more than one body, the system would still retain some form of democracy, although there is no direct relationship (no *feedback*, no opportunity to reply) between the voters of a small European country and the drafter of a Community regulation. The problem becomes more serious though, from the moment when the most important decisions on an economic, financial and developmental level are taken not by institutional bodies, as required by a democratic system, even if it is a rather loose network, but by powerful elites, by holding companies, multinationals, lobbies and the so-called 'market' – that is, by an accumulation of personal actions, technical consequences, emotional reactions, political will and particular interests that overlap in a very confusing manner and determine the fate of millions of people without any liability. Everything seems to happen because this is how the world turns and no one is able to oppose it: not the people taking to the streets, protesting, whose only result is, at best, to sensitize public opinion that is otherwise distracted by an excess of information;

not even the nation-state, which does not have the instruments needed to operate on a global scale and never had, since the issue had never been raised before.

As well as being physical, political, legal and economic, in compliance with the post-Westphalian model, borders have always maintained that balance of strength and relationships which now no longer exists.

The crisis of the state coincides with the crisis of the post-Westphalian model, whose certainties have been swept away by the opening of borders, by faster and faster exchanges of communications, by an economy on a global or supranational level and, not least, by a culture which is no longer restricted to a local level, and is deeply influenced by suggestions, information and comments from all over the world. The global village of McLuhan was created (or is being created) thanks to economic and cultural exchange, but at the expense of state-systems that are no longer in line with the changing times.

Where the state seeks to maintain its identity, even if only its cultural identity, unchanged (similar to that of the nation), it implodes violently. The trigger for this is mainly information, and therefore the awareness of change that leads to new needs.

Communications develop the imagination and expand desire. It is not so much the new technologies (mobile phones, the internet, social networks) that have caused the most recent libertarian processes (from the Arab Spring onwards), as information, knowledge and comparison with other realities. It is knowledge that makes us conscious of our differences with respect to others and produces desire and action. Technology only provides the necessary instruments. The imagination that triggers rebellion is fuelled by the widespread diffusion of new technologies that no state, even ones determined to maintain the integrity of their borders, can prevent. Force is not necessary. No power can halt the imagination when it is fuelled by knowledge and communication.

According to an old saying, 'knowledge is power', and knowledge in politics has always been crucial, especially when it was necessary to make decisions that would have caused problems for the population. For this reason, all libertarian movements have always insisted on educating the weaker social classes, to fight ignorance and, with it, the inability to access knowledge.

Governments have sought new alliances in the economy, which they have found to be an infallible instrument for allowing them to continue to exercise their power. The markets, virtual places – *non-places*, according to Marc Augé,[14] deprived of territoriality, impersonal and invisible – have now become the ultimate weapon of a supranational power that no longer needs the state in order to function. Their strength is undeniable for the very reason that it has been removed from political control, which somehow had to reckon with the population and implement a form of democracy – that is, of 'participation' in the people's collective. Removed from politics, power in the economic sense is disconnected from any bias or limitation of activity. It is free to express all its potential aggression in the pursuit of its primary objectives and is, therefore, an economic advantage.

Here, too, knowledge plays an important role. Knowledge of the economy, the mechanism of the markets and their operation would be essential to counteract power. Their strength is, once again, rooted in the people's ignorance: the operations and decisions that governments implement for and in relation to markets are passively accepted in a spirit of resignation that is very similar to fatalism. Without the possibility of reply or criticizing, there is no more than a dull and confused protest.

But power and politics are not two separate worlds travelling on different levels, without ever meeting. Their separation is not due to incompatibility, intolerance or misunderstanding. It's a separation of convenience, for operational needs, just as for couples who are separated only formally for tax purposes. Power and politics, united, went hand in hand when the state was an absolute monarch and the post-Westphalian model was still in force.

The separation has weakened politics and made it 'dependent' on the supranational economic power, with which, however, it has maintained good friendly relations for mutual benefit. In fact, despite having taken on an overwhelming, autonomous position, power needs politics in order to be fulfilled, to reach the most remote communities on the planet, where it can assert its economic imperatives. Without the acquiescence of politics, its task would be much more difficult; it would find difficulty in enforcing its regulations.

Since we are dealing with an economic power, it must be said that to achieve its purposes it becomes convenient and appropriate to apply the most liberal and competitive economic principles, the classic ones advocated by Adam Smith in the eighteenth century, in which the practice of 'laissez-faire, laissez passer', referring to the free movement of goods, is perfectly suited to the logic of globalization.

No constraints, no obstacles or customs duty for the exchange of products between any countries in the world – not to mention for the movement of money, which represents the symbolic value of goods and is accepted everywhere. Liberal or neoliberal principles – because they adapt the teachings of Smith, Ricardo and their followers to the needs of the contemporary world – are endorsed by most of the Western states that are suffering from the crisis of the post-Westphalian model of reference, and their slavish application is considered to be the only salvation from dissolution.

This self-preserving behaviour reveals the full horror of a perspective of future uselessness, the only – the last – opportunity to avoid becoming a state-counter that provides on-demand services to citizens, with no possibility of decision or control. To avoid this fate of becoming a simple entity of public service, without power, and without politics, the state clings to the only opportunity that is provided by the economic power to maintain a high level of function that justifies its existence and that of the 'grand commis' that animates and draws sustenance from it: adopting a neoliberal policy.

This operation allows the recovery of a certain control over the population, although as a result of decisions made elsewhere, for which the State becomes the bearer and interpreter at a local level.

A state, therefore, is now the executor of a higher power to which there is no opposition, but to which it is actually convenient to submit, for the maintenance of the *status quo*. Consequences for the population – daily, economic and social – will not be dealt with here, since they are easy to understand and are there for everyone to see – everyone who lives where neoliberalism has been put into practice. The fact is that, on the whole, the crisis of the post-Westphalian model has meant the withdrawal of the welfare state and most of the promises that modernity had made to its citizens.

The difficulty of management, the futility of corrective measures needed to deal with an emergency that has no end, are a consequence of this. Everyone tries to find local solutions (the only ones allowed) to global problems, when global solutions are required. In order for the state to return to carrying out its full institutional function, recovering the lost power to field policy, it should be a global state, able to intervene at the right level of authority.

Rather than face this problem, the current trend in all Western nations, to different degrees, is not to take it on.

The result is a sort of 'statism without a state', as defined by Balibar, which is a form of indirect 'governance', which relieves itself of any liability by transferring this burden to the individual. Behind this choice, this response to the crisis of the post-Westphalian model that cannot find an accessible replacement at the moment, there is the so-called 'neoliberal philosophy', which is more pragmatic than ideological in nature, in a world where the false certainties of ideology have been banned for some time. Neoliberalism is almost a natural decision, the self-protective instrument of a state which intends to hold firmly on to the reins of democracy and refers to representative democracy, at least formally, even though it has lost power. This is because neoliberalism, as the name implies, is anything but assertive, repressive and intrusive. It allows freedom of movement, but delegates to private sectors most of the responsibilities that were originally the state's. This is how we arrive at that completely new and unusual form of governing, with no accountability – that is to say, a 'state without a state', which is really postmodernism, or rather, post-postmodernism.

Zygmunt Bauman Hobbes' work was one among numerous efforts to lay theoretical foundations (rolled into one with the simultaneously pragmatic, functional and ethical legitimation) under the new entitlements and capacities bestowed on the sovereign by the formula *cuius regio eius religio* of the Westphalian settlement in its two phases – Augsburg (1555) and Osnabrück/Münster (1648). Among them, arguably the most influential at its time was Jean Bodin's *De la République, ou traité du Gouvernement*, published in 1576, four years after the massacre of St Bartholomew's Day which triggered the last – well-nigh the most gory, devastating and alarming – of the series of post-Reformation religious wars.[15] Bodin proclaimed 'la puissance absolue et

perpetuelle d'une Republique' (the absolute and perpetual power
of a Republic) – whereas, to unpack the meaning of the power's
'absoluteness' in chapters 8 and 10 of Book I he declared that 'the
sovereign Prince is only accountable to God'. While remaining a
staunch Catholic and consistently an adversary and a critic of the
Protestant tendency to seek the validation of state power in the
authority of the people, Bodin was at the same time a sturdy and
harsh opponent of Papal interference with the integrity of the
Prince's power. Intentionally or not, Bodin, just like Hobbes,
paved the way to the separation of the idea of princely power from
divine unction – a way leading eventually, in the course of subsequent centuries, to the substitution of 'natio' for the 'religio' in
the Westphalian formula. When suggesting that the Prince answers
to God only, Bodin, like Hobbes, managed to preserve for the
Prince the prerogative of the kind of inalienable and indivisible
sovereignty previously conferred solely by divine appointment,
while simultaneously eroding its dependency on ecclesiastical
appointment committees.

All the remaining 't's have been crossed and the rest of the 'i's
dotted by Carl Schmitt, pontificating that 'all significant concepts
of the modern theory of the state are secularised theological concepts . . . The omnipotent God became the omnipotent lawgiver
. . . The exception in jurisprudence is analogous to the miracle in
theology.'[16] Schmitt traced that passing of the relay baton down
to the rationalism of the eighteenth century, and particularly to
Rousseau's precept of 'imitating the immutable decrees of the
divinity' as the ideal of the legal life of the state (Schmitt quotes
with approval a 1902 Emil Boutmy suggestion that 'Rousseau
applies to the sovereign the idea that philosophers hold of God:
He may do anything that he wills but he may not will evil'); or
even further back, to Descartes, who wrote in a letter to Mersenne
that 'it is God who established these laws of nature just as a king
establishes laws in his kingdom'.[17]

It is symptomatic of, as well as crucial to, the modern notions
of state, power and sovereignty that Schmitt selected the equiva-
lence of *legal exception* and the *miracle* as the crowning argument
confirming his conclusion that all three have been but a secularized
variety of theology. The underlying assumption, tacit yet indispensable, is that the substance of designing or authoring laws is that
the discretion to choose lies in the hands of the designer or the

author and nowhere else; that it has been ultimately the will of one and the other that made all the difference between the specific design or the artifice actually chosen and the multitude of possible ones – conceivable though un-implemented.

The prerogative of choice applies both ways: what has been done can be undone. What has been chosen at will may be abandoned at will. What has been raised to the status of a universally binding norm can be suspended for a time, or its application may be confined to a less than universally binding norm. The designer/author can choose a law according to his will – and, according to his will – and it alone – he can make exceptions to its application. It is in that capacity of a sovereign to be unconstrained by the norm of his own creation, in his capacity of making exceptions, his entitlement and ability to bind or unbind, to impose a norm as much as an exception to the norm, that the substance of sovereignty lies. Ultimately, 'the legal order rests on a decision and not on a norm'.[18]

At the end of the day, it is the cancellation/suspension of a norm that supplies the conclusive evidence of sovereignty. It is not the prerogative of legislation and of making a norm binding that defines the sovereignty of power – the ultimate proof of sovereignty is the prerogative of *choice*: manifestation of the effective ability to *suspend* the law, *exclude* from law – and, all in all, to make *exceptions* to the norm. The ruler is a sovereign in as far as he has the power to make the choice between the two. Commitments may be binding because they rest on natural law, as Jean Bodin suggested; but in the case of emergency (by definition, an 'abnormal' condition positing abnormal challenges and calling for abnormal steps), 'the tie to general natural principles ceases', as Bodin also implied.[19] That was, after all, according to the Holy Scripture, the common expedient deployed whenever the lordship of the Lord was questioned and cast in doubt.

When Moses, sent on the mission to Pharaoh, feared that the Pharaoh would deny recognition to the divine origin of the message he carried, the Lord promised his messenger to 'stretch His hand and assail the Egyptians with all the miracles I shall work among them' (Exodus 3, 20-1). In order to 'imitate the *immutable* decrees of divinity', the earthly power – the sovereign – had to demonstrate his capacity to make his decrees *mutable*. Without this possibility, the capacity to make his decrees truly and unconditionally immutable would support sovereignty of the sovereign in the same way the noose supports the hanged man. It was the spectacular feat of *ignoring* the norm, not the humdrum chores aimed at sustaining its monotony, that brought to light – occasionally, yet memorably – the indomitable might of the sovereign. Machiavelli never tired of reminding his Prince that his feats of this kind needed to be repeated over and over again to keep them always fresh in the memory of those whom he ruled. Just like God's miracle-making capacity, so the Prince's ability to suspend laws and make exceptions to the rule makes him the source of his subjects' perpetual, overpowering and incapacitating uncertainty. We may guess that this is more or less what Machiavelli had in mind when instructing his addressee to count and rely more on his subjects' fear than on their love.

In his recently published thought-provoking study,[20] Ulrich Beck baptized Angela Merkel, German Chancellor and grand mistress of political gimmicks and subterfuge, as 'Merkiavelli': an updated embodiment, with a few minor adjustments demanded by the newly refurbished stage, of the Prince's awesome/fearsome knack for violating the normal and the routine and making them null and void being turned into a *sui generis* norm. The awareness that the monotony of the normal can be broken by the Prince at any moment, and that the choice of that moment is fully and truly in the Prince's power, and his power alone, must never be allowed to fade from his subjects' minds. The Prince's ability to counter the norm locates him apart from the rest of the universe, faithfully following Niccolò Machiavelli's advice. 'Merkel has positioned herself', writes Beck:

> between the Europe builders and the orthodox adherents of the nation-state *without* taking either side – or, rather, she keeps both options open . . . Merkiavelli's power is founded on her circumspection, the desire to do *nothing* . . . The strategy of denying assistance – *not* doing anything, not investing, making no credits and funds available . . . Hesitation as a means of coercion – that is Merkiavelli's method. This coercion is not an aggressive incursion of German money but the opposite. It is the threat of withdrawal, delay and the refusal of credit.[21]

This is it: coercion to surrender through the *threat of withdrawal*. Procrastinating, prevaricating, playing one's cards close to one's chest, resisting taking decisions and thereby leaving one's own hands untied and one's own intentions impenetrable, are newly found means of keeping other protagonists in a fog, their hands manacled and their capacity to make decisions – let alone to make their decisions prevail – paralysed. This keeps one's own options open while closing down the options of others; keeps one's own intended moves inscrutable, and therefore renders the calculations of others precocious or stillborn and altogether ineffective. All in all, this recasts the struggle for access to decision-making as a zero-sum game.

Ascribing Merkiavelli's tactics to her own unique acumen, finesse or craftiness, would, however, be uncomfortably (and misleadingly) close to overlooking the forest in which this particular phenomenon is but one of the most common trees. The threat of withdrawal and abandoning the game, while leaving the other players to stew in their own juices, has now become the most widely deployed and, most would agree, the most effective strategy of domination – one not at all confined to the game of politics alone or to just one school of thought in the art of the power struggle. It has its roots in the present-day unilateral breakage of previously reciprocal dependence between the dominant and the dominated. Whereas mutuality of dependence between bosses and the labour they hired led sooner or later – in the long term, if not the short or medium – towards the bargaining table, compromise and consensual (even if temporary) settlements, one-sided dependence renders consensus highly unlikely while facilitating nonconsensual, unilateral decisions on the part of the bosses, now no longer tied to a location and free to move elsewhere. Movements of capital are no longer confined to state boundaries; accordingly, the preferences of the local labour force and its bargaining powers no longer need to be taken into account – let alone such demands as may compromise the bosses' (or stock-holders') interests in moving to where the best action – that is, the highest profit – can be found. Nor do the locals need to be viewed as the 'reserve army of labour' to which capital owners are doomed to resort if business demands a rise in investments – and so the need to keep those prospective labourers in a good condition (reasonably well fed, clad, sheltered, educated and trained) no longer 'makes economic sense' to a capital that is now aware of belonging to Manuel Castells 'space of flows' – a space eminently immune to the vagaries of local politics. It is the new independence of capital roaming in the 'space of flows' (which, unlike the 'space of places', is not sliced into politically separate and notoriously inward-looking regions), a space full of profit opportunities which wandering/floating businesses would loathe – and so are utterly unlikely – to overlook, neglect and allow themselves to miss, that lies behind the unilateral withdrawal of business support for previously 'beyond left and right' commitment to the 'welfare state', as well as behind the global and intra-societal inequality currently growing at a pace not experienced in our part of the world since the nineteenth century. The present state of play promotes rugged competition, selfishness, social divisions and inequality with the same vigour and unassailable logic as the condition of 'mutual dependence' generated limitations to social inequality, strengthening of commitments, firm and lasting alliances and, all in all, human solidarity.

All this applies to nation-states as much as it does to business corporations. Although, in the case of 'Frau Merkiavelli' – who, after all, derives her power from the leadership of a territorially fixed political entity – the situation differs somewhat: the option of moving elsewhere if things at home get too hot for comfort is not open to her. However dominant the position of Germany in Europe may yet become, the dependence between Germany and Europe is and will remain reciprocal. Germany needs Euro and European unity as much as the weaker and less resourceful members of the Union need a strong and stable German economy. A strategy calculated to contrive more uncertainty, anxiety and fear in order to force the players into submission to the tune-setting monopoly of their pay-master, has its impassable limits; their transgression would prove devastating to the players, but also, in the last account, to the pay-master. Procrastination can't therefore be extended *ad infinitum*, uncertainty needs to be stopped short of the actors' total incapacitation and none of the participants can be allowed – or can afford – to leave the negotiating table; such a prospect is as horrifying and unacceptable to Cyprus and Greece as it is to Germany (and indeed to Britain, despite all of Cameron's posturing, calculated to placate the redneck faction of his party). The very same business interests which governments are expected to protect and promote in their role of local police precincts guarding the law and capitalist order would not allow things to go that far.

And so the protagonists and adversaries of all shades are bound to stay, willingly or not, by design or by default, in each other's company. They are destined to meet again – tomorrow, the day after tomorrow, at the end of the present round of budgeting talks and the beginning of the next. Whoever threatens to enact a different scenario would sooner or later have her or his bluff called.

Hobbes and the Leviathan

Carlo Bordoni   In the beginning there was a monster, Leviathan, a dark presence repressed from the public's evil consciousness. The image of Hobbes' Leviathan well represents the perspective of the composition of the modern state held by the inhabitants of the seventeenth century, who were tired of living in a world ruled by chance, disorder and corruption, tired of wars of religion, and an existence based on the primordial law of the survival of the fittest. Most importantly, they were eager to develop their business in a climate of mutual fairness.

Leviathan, as can be seen from the cover of the original edition of 1651, is a biological monstrosity that comes from the biblical tradition, its body formed by the bodies of human beings – a little like the portraits of Arcimboldo, whose features are made up of various objects or figures arranged in such a way as to create the optical illusion of it being a whole. In fact the compositions of Arcimboldo anticipate the taste of an age that feels the need to find a lost unity, collecting and arranging the various segments of society, and using them according to their functionality, to construct a balance, which is no longer a natural balance but 'humanized', i.e. bent to man's need to unify the forces, and comply with the laws, that make possible the composition of a civilized society.

Overcoming the 'natural' concept of society, Hobbes emphasizes the artificial character of his creation: 'Art goes yet further, imitating that Rationall and most excellent worke of Nature, *Man*. For by Art is created that great Leviathan called a Commonwealth, or State (in latine *Civitas*), which is but an Artificiall Man.'[22]

Leviathan is therefore a whole made up of many men, whose task it is to perform all the vital functions that are needed, and each has a different task depending on the position in which he is

located, and the functioning of the complex 'mechanism' is dependent upon the uniformity and regularity with which everyone does
his duty. This regularity of the whole is ensured by the head (the
'soul' of the Leviathan), i.e. the higher will of a 'sovereign' who,
as the etymology of the word clearly reveals, 'stands above'. He
decides, directs, moves and determines the actions of the whole
on behalf of everyone. Each member needs to adapt to this higher
will – otherwise, the risk is that the system will collapse.

In this innovative and extraordinary insight into the modern
state, we can find the full implementation of the principle of social
solidarity which is the basis of every society, even though the trite-
ness of the motto 'one for all and all for one' is subtly reinterpreted
(with a subtle semiological modification that is not always understood), referring not so much to the individual, as to the unity of
the whole. The One who provides for all, and who, therefore,
expects everyone to participate in all its sustenance (defence or
development), is clearly the state. The new modern entity pos-
sesses superhuman strength, much greater than that of the various
traditional authorities of the past – all the stronger because it does
not depend on divine investiture, on heredity of power or on
imposition by physical force, but on the will of everyone. Or at
least on that of the majority, which introduces the other corollary
identification of modernity, and that is the delegation of power
through the mechanism of collective representation – commonly
denoted by the term 'representative democracy'.

In the face of these considerations, it is clear that the modern
state, from its beginning in the figure of Leviathan, already contained in itself a form of massification, a significant source of
repression of individual autonomy, in contrast to the granting of
'economic' freedom for the middle class, who were allowed to
undertake productive and commercial activities at their own risk.
If this contradiction may appear inexplicable and inconsistent
with Leviathan's requirement of togetherness, it appears nevertheless to be legitimate and, in its own way, coherent when the 'clas-
sist' character of modernity becomes apparent. In other words, all
those (and they are the vast majority) who do not have the ability,
the will and the means to contribute to the economic, cultural and
civic development of the state, limit themselves to merely doing
their duty as citizen – and that is carrying out their activities in
their fields of competence, which means working together to

ensure the strength, defence, sustenance, and all the services necessary for the survival of everyone, and therefore also of the privileged minority. Their contribution is fundamental and, for this reason, must be guaranteed at all costs, either by persuasion or by force, so that the state – through its 'active' members (entrepreneurs, businesspeople, intellectuals, leaders) – can progress.

Not surprisingly, the policy of most industrialized countries – England first of all – was to take immediate action for the relief of social alienation, aimed at the poor, the unemployed, the homeless and destitute who crowded together on the edge of the industrial cities. The various 'Poor Laws', which were passed in succession between the sixteenth and nineteenth centuries, were concerned not so much with feeding and looking after them out of a sense of Christian charity – as the Church had done up to that time – as with reintegrating them into the production process. They were given the dignity of a job, not for a humanitarian purpose, but for a social purpose, so that they might contribute to overall advancement in their small way, without being dependent on the community – so much so that their destination, which before would have been the hospices or dilapidated shelters run by parishes, was now the factory, where they were required to do mandatory work. This was a form of cheap forced labour, which served to increase profits and lower production costs in the emerging industry.

Progress itself lay in the hands of a few, and in the sacrifice of all for the common good. The social differentiation is thus placed in principle on the idea of modernity, on which it feeds, by separating the 'sacrificed', those condemned to perform vital functions for Leviathan, from those who contribute in some other way, privileged by the opportunity to live a better life.

Obviously the principle of representative democracy descends from all this. Many, simply by virtue of the fundamental duty they are required to carry out in ensuring the continuity of the state, can only 'delegate' their decision-making power to others who are more experienced and dedicated to this task. This is a flawed democracy, as Rousseau observed, which can scarcely be distinguished from the constitution of Leviathan itself, based on partial surrender of the individual autonomy of those who are citizens of the state and therefore induced to carry out their duty and their function without questioning it. The aim of the modern state is, in part, determined by the questioning of this absolute principle:

the presumption to criticize the conduct of the executive, the same refusal to delegate individual power unless it can be monitored, the original sin of the prevalence of the self that endangers the balance that had been painfully achieved three centuries earlier.

The state is the great regulatory apparatus of modern nations. It was established as early as the fifteenth century and immediately demonstrated its ability to maintain control of the scattered population, lacking identity, that emerged from feudalism. Thomas Hobbes anticipates the establishment of the modern state in *De cive* (1642) and *Leviathan*, in which the multitude ('the dispersed mob') becomes a population in the union with the sovereign, by becoming subordinate to his unifying power. The people, together with the sovereign who represents them, become one. But the people partially give up their autonomy and their prerogatives of freedom in favour of the protection afforded by the state.

The modern state was created by virtue of this contract between the masses and the sovereign, with which they form a cohesive unit they can identify with. The concepts of nation, culture and traditions are implanted in a permanent way, and the principle of regionalization is affirmed – that is, the link with the territory which accommodates private property, the centre of personal interests and family life. All of this – with the addition of a common language, traditions, religion and culture – helps to turn the multitude, made up of individuals, into a single solid united body, which becomes a people. In exchange for the guarantee of legal rights, security, order and freedom to do business, the modern state establishes the explicit obligation to pay taxes and, implicitly, exercises social control. Rough and formal in its first application, it later became more and more refined with the setting up of records offices and registries of births, deaths, marriages and changes of residence; registration of property and land; documentation of property sales and inheritance; and trading, production and building permits.

The violent oppression of an intrusive state was subsequently replaced by conditioning – though no less invasive – of the individual's thought, as implemented through the hypnotic power of television and other mass media, whose form of communication from the top down – authoritative and persistent, from one to many, in a single direction – confirmed the massification and validation of the conscience, even more effectively.

Theodor W. Adorno, together with other members of the Frankfurt School, was right to criticize harshly the conditioning carried out by the mass culture (a process which he called the 'culture industry'), with the emergence of ephemeral artistic values, used only in order to support the market.[23]

The modern state was born, therefore, as a deeply undemocratic body – a noose-type arrangement that could not be negotiated or challenged. The sovereign had absolute decision-making power that came from a 'carte blanche' delegation. There is no need to mention the reasons for the delegation. They are those already mentioned with regard to the recognition of individual rights and private property, freedom to trade and take action and to enjoy the services provided by the state. In return for these benefits, citizens gave up their own authority and autonomy, in exchange for obligations, such as the payment of taxes, compulsory service in the event of war, obedience to the laws and regulations imposed. So far, there is no democracy. There is only a higher power (the modern state) with its organizational and functional needs and capabilities in support of its subjects and the sovereign.

This is not the same as in modern democracy. While, in Hobbes, both sovereign and state are identified, it is harder to identify the state within the heterogeneous set of representatives today. Here, representation is split; there is no longer only one sovereign, but a wide range of delegates, from which a democratic state is formed. It is easier to identify with one elected representative than with a variety of them, who have the task of forming the state, even when they are not part of the majority and they fight against the decisions of the majority. On the other hand, if all the delegates are themselves the state, that in itself justifies the difficulty in distinguishing between one party and another, between the majority and the opposition. Both move within the same system, both are the state and the ideological distinction that has characterized them until recently has been wiped out, erased forever from history.

Things get complicated when the introduction of democratic processes shatters the absoluteness of implicit delegation: the indivisible one who collects everything. Democratic needs call for implicit delegation (whether obtained by an act of force, by inheritance, by divine right or by execution of dynastic agreements) to be replaced by suffrage: the appointment by an absolute majority.

It is an innovation not to be undervalued because the sovereign is no longer invested with supreme authority, by a higher law, but by the will of the people. That is, from the bottom. Because it represents the state, the national unity, it is necessary to have the approval of the majority of the population.

The republican state is born. And it does not matter much whether the vote is direct or indirect, by the election of a group of representatives who will be responsible for electing the president of the Republic. And even if the President of the Republic (as in many countries, including Italy) is only a figure of guarantee, responsible for supervising compliance with the constitution and appointing the head of state, the principle remains the same: delegation is absolute and there is no right of withdrawal, at least for the period of the legislature.

Zygmunt Bauman The Hebrew 'Leviathan' is translated in the New English Bible (as indeed in modern Hebrew usages) as 'whale'. In the Book of Job (40, 41), it is referred to by God as one of the living proofs of the uniquely divine creative powers which Job, in common with all other humans, can't possibly match – only view with awe and obey. Of the Leviathan, God asks Job (a rhetorical question, if ever there was one): 'Can you pass a cord through its nose or put a hook through its jaw? . . . Will it enter into an agreement with you to become your slave for life? . . . Any hope of subduing him is false; the mere sight of him is overpowering.' You can hear God sneering, daring Job to accomplish feats obviously beyond human power and deriding Job, a member of the human race, for his hubris. Hubris of a single man, to be sure . . . Leviathan debunks and lays bare the futility of human (I repeat, a *single* human's) dreams of overpowering and subjugating the might of something not of his creation and which he is not capable of controlling, let alone forcing into servitude to him.

This particular biblical image inflamed the human imagination as few, if any, other mythical visions managed to. It has undergone, down the millennia, all sorts of recycling operations, and, as Carl Schmitt summarizes the results in *Der Leviathan in der Staatslehre der Thomas Hobbes* (1938), the wealth of its theological and historical interpretations is downright monstrous. But as you, Carlo, have rightly observed, the 'biological monstrosity' was nevertheless invested by Hobbes with a novel meaning in order to make it fit for the socio-political discourse the author intended. This novelty was to be conveyed by the cover drawing of the first edition, representing a huge man of arms composed of a multitude of tiny human figures (in other words, a 'fractal' drawing, reiterating the same structure at successive levels of the composition). The concept entailed by the drawing, as Hobbes explains in the seventeenth chapter of the second book ('On State'), is one huge and powerful person or body – the state – called into being through bringing and holding together a multitude of human individuals while providing a frame in which their togetherness is from then on contained – though, at the end of chapter 28, the referent of the 'Leviathan' in the title is narrowed down to the person of the 'Governor' ('Rector' in Latin), the holder of supreme power, the distributor of rewards and punishments that sustain the state as a totality cemented together thanks to its political unity. Thus he becomes like the Leviathan of whom God opined that it had no equal among earthly powers. As we know, the other mythical figure, that of Behemoth, stands, in Hobbes' toolbox of political metaphors, for the other force that Leviathan confronts and struggles to disarm and hold in submission: namely, for the force of anarchy, rebellion and internecine enmity which is embedded for all time in the 'natural state' of humans unless that state of nature is replaced or subdued and held in check by an 'artificial state' impersonated by the Leviathan, that mighty force composed of many singular and otherwise dispersed beings forced into peaceful coexistence. The morbid inclinations of humans are all the same never suppressed in full and unlikely ever to become extinct; superimposition of the Leviathan over the Behemoth is not a one-off task – it is a function to be diligently performed forever, without interruption. Leviathan is the sole remedy against the (inevitably short-lived, because it is self-destructive) rule of Behemoth – and so it is the *sine qua non* condition of continuing human existence on Earth. Quoting Thomas Carlyle, Schmitt reduces the human condition to a simple formula: anarchy plus police.

To express all this in a modern idiom: a political body is exposed to, and remains constantly under threat of being torn apart by, a centrifugal force of individualist self-assertion and a centripetal force of state-imposed and state-administered discipline. The two forces, however, are heterogenic: the first is 'natural' (i.e., not of human choice even if made by humans), the second 'artificial' (i.e., in addition to being human-made, also an outcome of a human choice). If one assumes that human self-centredness and aggression are inborn (indeed, biologically determined) pro-clivities, the need to launch a centripetal, integrating force to balance out their disruptive pressures is a simple deduction, as is the conclusion that such a need cannot be met by natural processes and can only – must – be imposed 'from outside' by compelling means – violent ones, if necessary.

The essential message of the *Leviathan* remains to this day an integral and perhaps irremovable part of common sense or doxa – a collection of beliefs which we think with, but seldom if ever think of. The prime role of the state is to enforce order; failure to do so makes it a 'failed state' (note that a state is not branded 'failed' for any other reason). How to achieve that purpose is, however, a contentious issue, as you, Carlo, rightly indicate.

Contemporary Leviathan, the modern state, was defined by Max Weber with reference to its monopoly on the means of coer-cion and their use. In practice, that monopoly boils down to the entitlement of the state's governing bodies – however they were selected, became entrenched and legitimize their right to enforce discipline on their subjects – to draw the line dividing coercion (legitimate violence) from violence (illegitimate coercion): the former is deployed in the name of the 'maintenance of law and order' – a task that includes primarily the elimination of the latter, classified as acts of violence. These are illegal and for that reason presumed to be order-disrupting and order-undermining. The right to draw such a demarcation line splitting applications of force into acts of legitimate coercion and of violence, remains throughout history the prime stake in the struggle for (political) power, as well as a principal – essentially indivisible and inalienable – attribute of (political) power-holders; for this reason, it tends to be, as a rule, 'essentially contested'.[24] The area surrounding that line remains a territory of frequent invasions and all too often gory battles, as well as of almost permanent reconnaissance sallies exploring the length to which the border posts may be pushed in one direction or another (most recently brought into the open by hotly contested court rulings in the State of Florida).

Two departures from the scheme of things as represented in the love–hate relationship between Behemoth and its offspring and

repressor Leviathan – possibly seminal departures – are occurring
at the moment. One concerns the way in which Leviathan's power
is exercised, and the second the purposes which its exercise is
aimed at attaining.

Joseph Nye has distinguished two kinds of power – 'hard' and
'soft' – though he concentrates his attention on international (or
more correctly inter-state) relationships.[25] In its general form,
though, the concept of the soft variety of power, described by Nye
as 'getting others to want the outcomes that you want' – a power
that 'co-opts people rather than coerces them' – is fully applicable
to our area of interest. As a matter of fact, one can suspect Nye
of deriving the idea of 'soft power', which he recommends the
leaders of the US should practise more earnestly than before on
the global stage (that is, a power targeted on tempting, seducing,
and obtaining the voluntary cooperation of their human objects,
rather than on forcing them to do what they would prefer not to
do), from already much more common – indeed ubiquitous and
daily – uses of that kind of power strategy not only by governments seeking their citizens' obedience, but also in the mechanism
of reproduction of the society of consumers. You have already
rightly pointed out the crucial role played, when the emergent
nation-states were confronted by the task of legitimizing themselves, by ideological indoctrination (in particular by the arousal
and beefing-up of the whole gamut of emotions, from benign
sentimental patriotism to chauvinistic extremes of nationalism,
resulting in the self-identification of citizens with the government
of their country, and the acceptance of an attitude of 'voluntary
servitude'). Please note, however, that this function, administered
and monitored centrally by governments during the nation-building era, has since then – along with a growing number of tasks
once upon a time jealously guarded by state governments as their
exclusive property and subject to their indivisible discretion – been
'outsourced' and 'contracted out' to market forces, which are
much more seasoned in the art of ideological indoctrination in its
current reincarnation as 'production of demand' – indeed, they
are the acknowledged grand masters of temptation and seduction.
The task of keeping patriotic motives on permanently lit or regularly rekindled burners has been relegated to private agencies
behind the anniversary spectacles or 'great events' (such as, most
recently, the birth of a baby into the third position in line to the

British throne) staged for nation-wide entertainment, or behind other emotion-releasing events such as the regular wars waged against the alien and conducted by a commercial proxy on football pitches or tennis courts.

But the shift to the 'soft' variety of power from the increasingly avoided 'hard' variety (which is old-fashioned and also unbearably costly, unlike its profit-generating successor) reaches much further than reforming the ways in which the orthodox functions of the Leviathan are tackled. As early as in his epochal study *La Distinction* (1984), Pierre Bourdieu[26] recorded the fateful drift from normative regulation to seduction, as well as from policing to arousing of desire – and, all in all, from coercion to PR. The overall focus of Bourdieu's study was the new yet increasingly widespread use of voluntary choices, instead of physical or economic coercion and psychological pressure, as the principal resource in obtaining a conduct conforming to one's intentions and set targets. Freedom of choice – an unduly neglected, though natural, human predisposition requiring no capital investments, and a self-propagating faculty of self-asserting individuals – has been found to be amenable to transformation from a handicap into an asset, from a costly risk into a reliable resource; in present-day accountancy it tends to be recorded more on the credit side of the calculation, instead of being entered on the debit side as it was under the 'hard power' regime. A most striking example of this tendency is the enlisting of surveilled and soon-to-be-surveilled human objects as the unpaid and fully voluntary agents of their surveillance. If old-style secret services had to collect information about the whereabouts and *modus operandi* of the potential 'dangerous elements' threatening law and order, which the services were called upon to protect with tremendous effort and at enormous expense to the state treasury, they can now confine themselves to digital processing of an enormous 'data base' which they would never be capable of collecting without entirely voluntary, unpaid and indeed enthusiastically keen assistance from all and any potential objects of targeted surveillance. We now live in a confessional society in which, metaphorically speaking, microphones are fixed in confessionals, those old-style sanctuaries of privacy and intimacy, and connected to loudspeakers installed on public squares – though also linked directly to servers storing the confessions for simultaneous and/or subsequent use by an unknown quantity of information-processors in an unknown number of data-gathering agencies pursuing their own objectives, unknown to the information-suppliers. For reasons I have tried to list elsewhere, we are all eager nowadays to supply, on our own initiative and at our own expense, all the details of our already undertaken or intended moves and deeds – information that is instantly added to the contents of the infinitely capacious servers of 'cloud internetting'. That such information is stored for eternal keeping and can be used at any time against our interests is by now a public secret – which, however, neither diminishes our dedication to self-spying nor reduces, let alone stems, the inflow of information into the files stored in Leviathan's security offices.

Let me signal briefly another seminal departure in the Leviathan–Behemoth relation. As in Jeremy Bentham's suggestion, raised by Michel Foucault to the level of a general theory of power, the Leviathan's technique of domination over endemically unruly Behemoth (unruly, let's recall, due to the anarchic predispositions of the human individuals composing it) took a 'panoptical' shape: the maximal reduction of the range of choices left to the human objects of normative regulation and behavioural control, coupled with incessant surveillance for the sake of the instant punishment of all and any deviations from the imposed routine. Among the best-known, most meticulously documented and most widely debated manifestations of the Panopticon style of domination and control were the techniques of time-and-motion measurement designed by Frederick Taylor, or Henry Ford Sr's conveyor belt running along the assembly line.

The codification of techniques combining in the panoptical variety of domination and control was accomplished by Max Weber in his depiction of the ideal-typical 'bureacracy' – an arrangement meant to assure the rationality of the actions and interaction of all those involved. That ideal type was focused on the elimination from the choice-making processes of all and any factors considered irrelevant to the objective to which a given bureaucratic organization was dedicated – and particularly of such factors as emotions, individual loyalties, personally held beliefs or values cherished by the employees. What all these measures amounted to was an effect similar to that expected of the Panopticon: replacement of variegated motives and commitments guiding human choices by a single hierarchy of super- and sub-ordination, sewn and held together by streamlined and strictly uni-directional channels of communication – commands flowing from the top of bureaucracy down to the bottom level and reports drawn in the opposite direction. The ideal model for the rational conduct of human affairs held no room for individuality, nor indeed for an individual more complex and multi-faceted than her/his assigned role inside the organization.

New managerial philosophy and practice no longer treats that model as ideal. Rationality, it is now deemed, is hardly a foolproof recipe for success in the liquid-modern world of contingency, volatility, fluidity, endemic uncertainty and high risk. Scanning the vast and borderless, constantly changing in size and contents, expanse of opportunities notorious for their confusing habit of appearing with little or no warning and running away or vanishing if they aren't instantly seized – a scanning guided by intuition, impulse and audacity, rather than by prolonged and systematic in-depth studies – appears much more promising. Sticking to the rules, following the established criteria and restricting vision to the narrow, bordered and fenced-off field defined a priori as 'relevant to the task', seems on the other hand, to be a recipe for disaster. If the wisdom of orthodox bureacratic management, which relied on stability and continuity of surroundings and rested accordingly on the production and strict observance of routine, called for learning and memorizing, the wisdom of the new management, which is aware of operating in volatile and essentially unpredictable circumstances, calls for perpetual questioning of received knowledge, rejection of routine, irregularity and forgetting. Initiative, imagination, novelty and daring are the virtues of today. Come back variety and peculiarity from the exile to which the pursuit of rationality sentenced you! As for their antonyms, uniformity and conformity, they are no longer welcome – it is their turn to seek asylum.

In such an environment, personal peculiarities, including bizarre and unclassifiable idiosyncrasies that were once banned from the office and had to be left in the cloakroom on entering the building, come to be seen as the most precious of assets and the most promising and profitable capital. Pursuit of success requires them to be cherished, not fought and smothered. Wings need to be spread wider, not cut. It is no longer employees who follow the rules and go through the motions who are in demand, but self-composed, self-managed and self-confident, boisterous and unconventional individuals. The phenomenon of 'individuality', which was once frowned upon, looked askance at, viewed with a mixture of derision and fear and, all in all, treated with suspicion as a potential menace to the order of things, is now rehomed in the family of most desirable resources and most praiseworthy and enviable qualities. In the economy and state, as well as life politics, in the liquid-modern setting, individuality replaces order, and individualization elbows out ordering on the agenda of topmost objectives and the list of uppermost concerns.

One wonders to what extent the Hobbesian Leviathan vs Behemoth imagery has retained its value. After all, a major, well-nigh defining, attribute ascribed to the Behemoth was that of the breeding ground of disorder, aggression and anarchy, all stemming from the selfish and unruly nature of humans in their capacity as individuals instead of units holding an assigned place in a structured, hierarchically organized and managed whole (community/society, nation, state); while the major, indeed defining, attribute ascribed to the Leviathan was the mission of, and daily engagement in, subduing and keeping under control the chaos perpetually emanating from the compound of Behemoth. In the simplest of terms, the calling and the *raison d'être* of Leviathan was the suppression of the individuality bred by Behemoth.

And let me mention briefly one more fateful departure that hints at a rethinking of the nature of the Leviathan vs Behemoth opposition, or the state vs society relation for which that allegory stands.

In *Legitimationsprobleme im Spätkapitalismus*, a study published in 1973 in the twilight of the society of producers, when the first signs were appearing of the impending dawn of the society of consumers, Jürgen Habermas famously and memorably presented the capitalist state as aimed at continuous reproduction of the essential building blocks with which the capitalist society is constructed, and constantly re-supplied and reinvigorated in the course of its self-reproduction.[27] Those essential building blocks are the (regular) encounters between capital and labour culminating in the transaction of buying and selling. The prime function of the capitalist state, Habermas averred – indeed the function that makes it a *capitalist* state (that is, one that serves the reproduction of society in its capitalist form) – is to secure the necessary conditions for such encounters to keep on taking place. And the two closely interconnected conditions that must be met for the encounters to happen regularly and achieve their purpose are that capital is able to pay the price of labour, and that the labour offered for sale is in a suitable condition to make the purchase attractive to capitalists – its prospective buyers. Now, however, deep in the consumer society, it looks as if the function of the capitalist state is the provision of an altogether different 'essential building block' of the capitalist edifice that has recently replaced its predecessor as described by Habermas: the meeting of customer with commodity. The conditions for the purchase/sale transaction to take place regularly and with sufficient frequency now consist in ensuring that the customer is in a position to pay the price of the commodity on offer, while the commodity is sufficiently attractive to commend itself at that price.

Notes

1 E. J. Hobsbawm, 'Nations and Nationalism in the New Century', preface to *Nationen und Nationalismus: Mythos und Realität seit 1780*, Campus, 2005.
2 É. Balibar, *Cittadinanza*, trans. F. Grillenzoni, Bollati Boringhieri, 2012.
3 Z. Bauman, *Community: Seeking Safety in an Insecure World*, Polity, 2000.
4 Balibar, *Cittadinanza*, p. 39.
5 Ibid., p. 136.
6 Hobsbawm, 'Nations and Nationalism in the New Century'.
7 W. Brown, 'Neoliberalism and the End of Liberal Democracy', in *Edgework: Critical Essays on Knowledge and Politics*, Princeton University Press, 2005, pp. 37–59.
8 J. Gray, *False Dawn: The Delusions of Global Capitalism*, Granta Books, 2009.
9 See H. Welzer, *Climate Wars: Why People Will Be Killed in the Twenty-first Century*, trans. P. Camiller, Polity, 2012, p. 176.
10 J. M. Coetzee, *Diary of a Bad Year*, Vintage Books, 2008, p. 79.
11 Ibid., p. 119.
12 J. Habermas, *The Postnational Constellation: Political Essays*, Polity, 2000, p. 76.
13 A. Appadurai, *Modernity at Large: Cultural Dimensions of Globalization*, University of Minnesota Press, 1996.
14 M. Augé, *Non-Places: Introduction to an Anthropology of Supermodernity*, trans. J. Howe, Verso, 2009.

15 J. Bodin, *On Sovereignty* (1576), ed. and trans. J. H. Franklin, Cambridge University Press, 1992.

16 C. Schmitt, *Political Theology: Four Chapters on the Concept of Sovereignty*, trans. G. Schwab, University of Chicago Press, 1985, p. 36.

17 Ibid., pp. 46–7.

18 Ibid., p. 10.

19 Ibid., p. 8.

20 See U. Beck, *German Europe*, trans. R. Livingstone, Polity, 2013, pp. 45ff.

21 Ibid., pp. 49–50.

22 T. Hobbes, *Leviathan* (1651), Penguin, 1985, p. 81.

23 M. Horkheimer and T. W. Adorno, *Dialectic of Enlightenment* (1947), trans. J. Cumming, Verso, 1997.

24 A term introduced in W. B. Gallie, 'Essentially Contested Concepts', *Proceedings of the Aristotelian Society*, 56 (1956), pp. 167–98, and unpacked by the author as referring to the 'concepts the proper use of which inevitably involves endless disputes about their proper uses on the part of their users'. As John Gray rightly commented (see J. Gray, 'On Liberty, Liberalism and Essential Contestability', *British Journal of Political Science*, 8, 4 (October 1978), pp. 385–402), disputes around issues classified as 'essentially contested' 'cannot be settled by appeal to empirical evidence, linguistic usage, or the canons of logic alone'.

25 J. Nye, *Soft Power: The Means to Success in World Politics*, Public Affairs, 2004.

26 P. Bourdieu, *Distinction: A Social Critique of the Judgement of Taste* (1979), trans. R. Nice, Routledge, 2006.

27 J. Habermas, *Legitimationsprobleme im Spätkapitalismus*, Suhrkamp, 1973.

2

Modernity in Crisis

The status of knowledge is altered as societies enter what is known as the postindustrial age and cultures enter what is known as the postmodern age.

Jean-François Lyotard[1]

The promises withdrawn

Carlo Bordoni Modernity withdrew its promises. Postmodernity underestimated them, even derided them, filling up the gap with glitter, images, colours and sounds; replacing substance with appearance and values with participation.

The first promise to be withdrawn was that Enlightenment idea of security, provided by the prospect of controlling nature. The great certainties of a technology that can prevent and avoid natural catastrophes collapsed in the face of the fact that nature will not be bent, in addition to the occurrence of so-called 'moral catastrophes' caused by man, which are often much more serious than the natural ones, in a sort of competition as to who is more skilled in the field of destruction.

After the Lisbon earthquake of 1755, the spirit of modernity had tried to subordinate disasters and their unpredictability to the power of reason, through the work of prevention and on a scientific basis.

'For I showed men how they were the cause of their own unhappiness and, in consequence, how they might avoid it', writes Rousseau to Voltaire in his famous letter on the Lisbon disaster, laying the foundations of a new spirit that desacralizes nature, removing it from divine will and entrusting it to the hands of man.[2] Natural disasters are transformed into moral ones because man becomes responsible for them, having at his disposal all the instruments that science offers him in order to avoid them. It is no longer a question of chance. What happens is never unpredictable: there are always breaches, carelessness, incompetence, omissions, which have not prevented the occurrence.

It is the carelessness of man that makes catastrophes *moral* and, therefore, avoidable. This promise, a fascinating and liberating vision of a world which emerged from fatalism, obscurantism, and seemed to herald the absolute dominion of man over nature, was bound to fail miserably with the crisis of modernity. This was a promise more betrayed than withdrawn, if almost three centuries later, scientists and expert volcanologists, in the face of the tragic events that disrupt the earth, confess that 'earthquakes cannot be predicted'. It was also a declaration of surrender in the face of nature, a step backwards with respect to Rousseau, and another mortal wound to the idea of progress on which the hope of a better world was based.

But it was not the only promise to be withdrawn. Others have suffered the same fate, or are about to. The idea of progress as a continuous development, linked to an ever wider availability of products and therefore consumerism – an optimistic idea on which much of the teleological assumption of happiness through having, rather than being, is based.

Now even the ultimate promise, painstakingly acquired after centuries of union disputes, political battles and costly conquests, is called into question: the existence of the social guarantor.

This involves all the measures provided for by the State as part of the overall reciprocal agreement with the citizen, to safeguard his health, his right to work, essential services, social security, retirement, old age.

With a sense of helplessness, we witness the piece-by-piece dismantling of the social or welfare systems, but this further example of *deconstruction* resulting from modernity does not produce widespread alarm. Indignation, despite Stéphane Hessel's exhortation, remains limited, almost a personal problem, surrounded by the general indifference of a community that is increasingly bewildered and confused, worried about surviving a temporary crisis and salvaging what can be saved.[3] Like in a wartime economy, or a state of emergency, in which everyone looks out for number one, trampling on others and clinging to the nearest lifeline.

Social guarantees that until a few decades ago were the backbone of individual existence are phased out, diminished or emptied of meaning. The certainty of employment has been called into question by terminable contracts, adding to the phenomenon of the insecurity of temporary employment. Cuts in public spending limit essential services, from the right to education to health care, whose insufficiency affects the quality, rapidity and adequacy of care for the chronically ill, the weak and the less able. The need for a *spending review*, to save – as opposed to the long-term habit of wasting resources, for which the political system was responsible in the first place – calls into question the legitimacy of acquired rights, sanctioned by law and by common sense, including the certainty of a given retirement age, the right to receive a *decent* living allowance and severance pay for those who have worked a lifetime. Everything has become debatable, questionable, shaky, destined to remain standing or to be wiped out with a stroke of the pen in consideration of urgent needs, budget problems, and compliance with European regulations.

Behind this philosophy of uncertainty, behind the liquidation of the welfare state, which not only affects Europe, but is rampant to a greater or lesser extent at a global level, lies the neoliberal belief that everyone should provide for themselves, without burdening others with their needs and their shortcomings.

This is an attitude which is actually not at all 'social', unworthy of any group of people that wants to call itself a community, and has its roots in a primordial conception of modernity, exalted by the bourgeois: the individual free from constraints and influences (hence *liberal*), capable of making his own way (the *self-made man*), of climbing the social ladder and succeeding thanks to his own capabilities, the ruthlessness of his behaviour and his own personal intuition. It is an attitude still apparent, in some ways, in American society, where until recently health care was considered a 'supplement' reserved for those who could afford the cost of private insurance.

In neoliberal logic, the economistic principle prevails, according to which every action, every concession, every service must bring in its own profit, the cost of which should be borne by those who use it and not be spread over the entire community, whose only obligation is to contribute collectively to maintaining the apparatus of the state. The strict application of this rigorous principle, the only one that enables the enormous public debt to be reduced, produces disastrous consequences in terms of social justice, as is clearly evident where it is applied. While in the United States, during the Obama administration, a process was inaugurated to limit the most devastating effects of neoliberalism (starting with health care), in Europe the first blows can be felt of a reverse economic policy. It is true that the neoliberal bending of the measures already taken earlier will fully come to fruition when the first social security measures expire – for example, shrinking retirement pensions calculated according to the contributory system, or raising the retirement age – but there are now worrying signals and tangible proof that the effects of the progressive cuts can already be felt.

The most odious aspect of this manoeuvre, which was announced with the solemnity of people taking courageous decisions for the salvation of the world, is that these decisions invariably affect the weak, those who cannot defend themselves, and all those who have no other choice but to suffer, because the injustice lies in the generality and the totality of the restrictions, despite their apparent equilibrium, and their apparent democracy. It seems to be a contradiction in terms, yet subtracting from everyone to the same extent (or making more people pay more, in proportion) is an act of blatant injustice, because it hurts the most disadvantaged, the poor and the needy. This perverse effect, if not corrected properly, creates a split in society, separating the privileged classes from the vast majority of the population, who are the ones affected by the recession.

This separation is already in place and is slowly beginning to change the habits, consumption and lifestyles of millions of people. It was not difficult to see it coming. It is not difficult now to know what the consequences will be in the future. Even those who have theorized about it, who are applying their theories, hiding it behind the label of the crisis to be overcome, cannot know what the consequences will be. There is a suspicion, therefore, that somebody wants this: a crisis induced, deliberately implemented to obtain the precise result that we all fear.

Another aspect to be considered is related to the temporary nature of crisis, that is to say, to its singularity as it is perceived by everyone as an event of limited duration, which we can soon leave behind and without too much damage, thanks to the drastic measures taken to deal with it. Sacrifices are more easily endured if they are short-lived, if the purpose and end are seen in the near future. However, crises, even induced ones, can no longer be considered temporary. They represent a permanent *status*, endemic, in the liquid world. In fact, they are its key feature exactly because of the lack of economic and existential stability we are experiencing. So, just as we live in an insecure society, where uncertainty prevails, we also live in a perpetual state of crisis, dominated by repeated attempts at adjustment and adaptation, which are continually challenged.

There is no way out of crisis, ever. We could say, to console ourselves, to give order to the reality we experience and to understand the inconvenience, that we are forced to face an unfortunate series of crises that happen one after the other, instead of recognizing that we are immersed in one single great crisis, as a consequence of the end of modernity.

The current crisis is not only striking Europe, it is not only an economic crisis: it is a profound crisis of social and economic transformation, which has its roots in the past. It comes from way back in time. To understand it, and accept it, we must go back to its causes, connecting it to the end of modernity and the painful passage through a controversial period of adjustment that has been defined as postmodernity. But the effects of the epochal derangement that changed man and unhinged modern society, whose model we still cling to with yearning, are meant to last forever.

Zygmunt Bauman   I am not sure I would go all the way with your thesis of modernity abandoning (or even having already abandoned) its promises. What you list under the heading of 'promises' were in fact *strategies* that were considered/hoped/expected to bring those promises to fulfilment. The promises themselves have remained amazingly steady – indeed astonishingly immune to the cross-waves of history, emerging largely unscathed from each successive crisis of faith. What was abandoned – and many times over – were favoured strategies, as well as the *models of a 'good society'* designed eventually to crown the effort of pursuing them resolutely and staunchly. What was 'abandoned' as well, and in my view most seminally, were the youthful *illusions* of modernity: most importantly, the illusion that the failure of any one strategy, or even of an infinite number of strategies, is not a final proof of the promise's futility, and that a foolproof strategy will eventually be found and any evidence to the contrary is but a transient, momentary hiccup caused by science and its practical arm, technology, lagging behind the task at hand. That conviction has indeed been questioned, eroded, perhaps abandoned altogether, or at least put on a back burner.

Few minds – if any – are nowadays busy designing the blueprints of a 'good society' – that ultimate station on the long road to perfection and the last stand in the war which modernity with all its youthful hubris declared on contingency, accidents, ambiguity, ambivalence, uncertainty – and, all in all, on the equally irritating and humiliating opacity of human fate and prospects. And two changes have occurred to the kinds of strategy that are currently likely to be sought and designed. Firstly, they are no longer comprehensive, no longer targeted on the overall shape of society – they are focused instead on the individual, and individually monitored and controlled parts of the order of things. This does not mean that the era of utopian thinking is over – it just means that the original gardener-style utopias have by and large been elbowed out and replaced by hunter-style utopias, offering a vision of a comfortable, secure niche carved out, fenced in and 'gated' for individual enjoyment inside a still (for a long, perhaps infinite, time) malfunctioning, poorly controlled, insecure and altogether inhospitable world. Secondly, having turned allergic at radical because total, all-embracing projects, modern spirit is now following Karl Popper's recommendation to render progress 'piecemeal', taking one thing at a time and, as far as the distant bridges are concerned, not worrying about crossing them until they have been reached.

So, yes: illusions have been abandoned (or, more to the point, ideas held once to be truths have been reclassified as illusions), whereas the strategies that go on being embraced, abandoned and replaced (all at an apparently accelerating pace) have changed their remit and their character. But I would stop there: modern *promises* are still alive and well. What is more, it is precisely thanks to their persistence and power of attraction/seduction that the discredited and abandoned strategies are as a rule promptly replaced by new ones, whose production goes on unabated.

There is one more point of disagreement. Speaking of modernity's promises, you suggest that 'postmodernity underestimated them, even derided them'. Whatever you call the present chapter of modern history – postmodernity, late modernity, reflexive modernity, second modernity, liquid modernity or any other of the many names thus far suggested – this chapter does not tell the story of modern promise being undermined or derided, but, on the contrary, of it being resurrected, reinvented, reincarnated, dusted-off and dressed in a recycled and refreshed or brand-new attire, as well as shuttled to a new rail track adjusted for high-speed vehicles. I am even tempted to say that it is in our times that the original promise of modernity has reached its thus far fullest fruition.

The ambitions (and so also the promises) of modernity were in fact summed up already in 1486 by Pico della Mirandola, a young man of just twenty-three at the time – as would and should only be expected of a prophet of a new age which was still out of sight, yet already germinating and gathering force beyond the horizon. Those promises were listed in his famous 'Oration', which was destined to inspire the Renaissance dress-rehearsal for the modern era and so also, indirectly, some time later, to assist at the birth of the modern spirit. Let me quote once more his oft-quoted words, which young Pico put in the mouth of – who else? – The Almighty, as he addressed – who else? – Adam, the first man:

> He made man a creature of indeterminate and indifferent nature, and, placing him in the middle of the world, said to him 'Adam, we give you no fixed place to live, no form that is peculiar to you, nor any function that is yours alone. According to your desires and judgment, you will have and possess whatever place to live, whatever form, and whatever functions you yourself choose. All other things have a limited and fixed nature prescribed and bounded by our laws. You, with no limit or no bound, may choose for yourself the limits and bounds of your nature. We have placed you at the

world's centre so that you may survey everything else in the world. We have made you neither of heavenly nor of earthly stuff, neither mortal nor immortal, so that with free choice and dignity, you may fashion yourself into whatever form you choose. To you is granted the power of degrading yourself into the lower forms of life, the beasts, and to you is granted the power, contained in your intellect and judgment, to be reborn into the higher forms, the divine.

Pico saw necessary to add but a handful of words of his own to God's blend of promise and command: 'Imagine! The great generosity of God! The happiness of man! To man it is allowed to be whatever he chooses to be!'

The promise of modernity (and, since it was God's invention and God's decision, whatever is promised in it is a verdict with no right to appeal) was, to follow Pico's manifesto, human freedom to self-create and self-assert: humans being free to choose their preferred mode of being-in-the-world. All forms are up for grabs. No choice is a priori excluded; not one has been cast by divine command beyond human reach. Note that the container bursting with choices has no lid, but has no bottom either: it includes descending to the level of beasts as much as it does the chance of rising to the level of the divine. The genius of Pico gathered fairly early on that there can be no freedom of self-creation without the possibility of blunder, and no opportunity for success without the risk of defeat – the truth that was to be challenged or ignored a couple of centuries later by the up-and-coming, young and boisterous modernity, which tried to exorcise the demon of risk and remove the fly of uncertainty from the barrelful of freedom, as well as to accomplish that feat by presenting the unstoppable march of progress, that unswervingly uni-linear movement from good to better, as being no less predetermined and final – indeed as obligatory and irrevocable – as freedom to choose itself. Progress was assured in advance and irreversible: one of those illusions destined to be lost or abandoned in the course of modernity's coming-of-age.

All the same, Pico's vision of times to come appears less illusory to us – wise as we are after the fact, disenchanted and embittered – than it would appear to the congregation of the Church of Progress in the eighteenth and nineteenth centuries. If something in Pico's eulogy prompts us to raise our eyebrows, it is his unalloyed enthusiasm for the package deal called 'freedom', warts and

all, complete with the collateral damages of liberation. Whenever
the issue of freedom is debated in our own time, one can expect
doubts, fears, worries and dark premonitions to be expressed
more often than bright hopes – let alone the certainty of blessings
and benefits to come. Read the latest statements by John Gray,
summing up the present mood, whether explicitly voiced, or, for
one reason or another, remaining subterranean, reluctant to show
itself in the open: 'By toppling the tyrant, people are free to tyran-
nize each other'; 'To think of humans as freedom-loving, you must
be ready to view nearly all of history as a mistake'; in Gray's view,
liberal crusaders for human rights 'are convinced that all the world
longs to become as they imagine themselves to be . . . Liberal civilization rests on a dream.'[4] You may easily accuse Gray of pushing
his criticism too far in the opposite direction – from unclouded
optimism to unmitigated and unremitting despair, and from a
staunch, unshakeable faith in the endemically progressive nature
of history to an equally staunch and quite unambiguous presenta-
tion of the very same history as an unending series of hopelessly
zigzag- or pendulum-like meanderings between the poles of good
and evil. But it is not so easy to deny the sharpness of Gray's sight
and hearing: he makes few if any mistakes when it comes to spot-
ting, plotting and reporting current shifts and drifts in the public
mood, however precocious and ill formed they may yet be (for the
time being, and no one can say how long for) or be believed to
be (if noticed at all) by common opinion. And one can't deny his
courage: it takes a stout heart and nerves of steel to call things by
their true names, however 'politically incorrect' their names might
currently sound. Moreover, one can't impute to Gray the misdeed
of being 'in a state of denial' about modernity's promise. As a
matter of fact, the direction in which people tend, in rising
numbers, to veer, is towards a loyal continuation and legitimate
offspring of that promise.

Pico waxed lyrical at the vision of the ultimate freedom which
he himself, together with his contemporaries, never had the chance
of experiencing first hand. Because it came of age when the *ancien
régime* was slowly yet relentlessly dissipating and the Lisbon catas-
trophe had just occurred – a time when every plank in the familiar
frame of human existence was rotting and falling apart one by
one, when everything solid melted into air and everything sacred
was profaned – the modern promise focused first on a collectively

provided and guarded security, and on freedom second, all too often a distant second. This was, after all, a promise to replace chaos with order, uncertainty with self-assurance, complexity with simplicity, and opacity with transparency. It was a promise of 'freedom *from*' (the vagaries of nature, blows of fate, enmity of neighbours) rather than of 'freedom *for*' (for gaining 'whatever place to live, whatever form, and whatever functions you yourself choose', as Pico imagined). The common denominator in both versions – the factor of continuity in this discontinuity – was the promise to take world affairs, including the human condition, under human management – and through it, under the rule of Reason, that synonym of order. One had to wait another couple of centuries for Sigmund Freud to proclaim that 'civilization' (a synonym of man-made and man-managed order) is a trade-off between security and freedom: not a cooperation between them but a zero-sum game. This is a conflict that is utterly unlikely ever to grind to a halt, and having promised to provide security *and* freedom, the two *sine qua non* conditions for a humane human existence, human management of the world proved capable, as had happened under previous managements, of supplying one *or* the other – hardly ever together and never in well-balanced, un-contentious proportions. What neither the apostles of freedom nor the advocates of order realized or admitted seems now all but obvious: that security and freedom are amenable to lasting reconciliation no more than are the desires to have a cake and eat it.

It transpired, moreover, that the objectives put on the agenda, and the zeal with which the managers of order pursue them, tend to bring results opposite to those overtly proclaimed. One misses most what one has lost or believes that one lost; and now that more and more water has flown under the bridges, the memory of reasons for which the lost property was set afloat in the first place fades. The unprepossessing aspects of that property, which inspired and pressed one's ancestors to throw it overboard, are forgotten, or if not entirely forgotten then at least played down to a point where the passions of the predecessors become all but incomprehensible to their successors. What could such minor inconveniences of the past matter, the latter ask, when compared with the horrors to which we are nowadays exposed?! However great the discomfort those inconveniences caused them, it must surely have been a price worth paying for what they enjoyed and we have been deprived of? Neither hatred and fear of freedom, nor hatred and fear of coercively imposed order are inborn traits of the human species or 'lie in human nature'. It is just that what we call 'progress' is not a uni-directional, linear movement but like a pendulum, with its energy drawn alternately from the desire for freedom (once we start to feel that security is excessively, unendurably intrusive and oppressive) and the desire for security (when we start to feel that freedom is an excessively, unendurably risky business producing too few winners and far too many losers).

The story of the last century and (so far) of the present one provides an object-lesson in that rule. By the end of the nineteenth century, libraries were filled to the brim with scholarly studies written by the Fukuyamas of the day and re-presenting history as one long march towards freedom, ending in its final and irreversible triumph. Shortly afterwards came the drowning of the forward-looking, allegedly indestructible, civilization that had been established once and for all, in the rivers of blood flowing over the battlefields of Europe, with an aftermath of prospectless unemployment and impoverishment for the masses and collective bankruptcy for the middle classes, sprinkled but sparingly with a few flash-in-the-pan triumphs which were promptly lost by gamblers on the stock exchange. What was the reaction? The deprived classes were pulverized into the masses and became all too eager to answer the calls of self-appointed saviours (of nations, races or classes) and to march joyously and obediently, with songs and torches, into totalitarian prisons to be shortly recycled into military barracks, while the middle classes danced around the auto-da-fe of their cherished liberties.

Dreams of less chaos and more order survived their totalitarian prelude, however, for just a 'thirty glorious years' of war declared on human misery, fear and deprivation under the banners of the 'welfare state' or 'état providence'. After those years, a call was heard on both shores of the Atlantic – coming from the generations emboldened by growing up with collective, community-endorsed insurance against individually suffered misfortunes. They felt firm in the saddle and were armed with a self-confidence their parents had no chance of acquiring: 'Come back, liberty, all is forgotten and forgiven.' Another thirty years or so passed by, and the delights of unbridled freedoms were followed by the headaches and nausea of the morning after: the need to repay retrospectively the exorbitant costs of a credit-triggered and credit-fed consumerist orgy, massive and again prospectless unemployment – made this time even more humiliating by the shameless public display of rampant inequality: the richest 1 per cent grasping 90 or more per cent of the nationally added value.

What we see with increasing clarity when looking around, and what probably inspired John Gray to jump with undue haste to his overly generalized conclusions, is a landscape after an orgy. Its beneficiaries-turned-victims have come to see freedom as a breeding ground for injustice and for the horrors of inadequacy, impotence and humiliation, while finding themselves left to their own individually held defences, which are jarringly insufficient for fighting back collectively produced menaces and miseries. They are also, unsurprisingly, increasingly inclined to view as major villains of the piece the state-political elites, recalcitrant and self-effacing as they are, keeping stubbornly aloof and programmatically uncommitted and non-interfering, washing their hands of their citizens' misery. Those elites (whether they are currently in power or in opposition to the current leaders) also seem to them to be living on another planet and speaking in an alien language. What those elites talk about, if it can be understood at all, concerns a reality starkly different from the one they know firsthand: obviously, elite concerns are not our concerns, our worries are not their worries. Little wonder that, to a growing number of neglected citizens, freedom looks uncannily like what the rich need to get richer and to push all the rest deeper into their misfortune.

Are we nearing, for the second time in recent history, a condition ripe to be exploited by demagogues who are sufficiently inane, self-deluded or arrogant to promise a short-cut to happiness and to blaze a trail right back to the lost paradise of security on condition that we surrender the liberties that are already abhorred by, and intensely unwelcome to, their possessors, and so also our right to self-determination and self-assertion? It is all too evident that there is no shortage of adventurers eager to do just that from the growing profusion and rising volume of calls of the 'Trust me, follow me, and I'll save you from the misery in which you would otherwise sink even deeper than you wallow now' type. The latest novelty is that these calls (still only a few – but how long will that last?) are coming from presidential and prime-ministerial offices.

For now at least, these tendencies are particularly salient and shocking in the post-communist countries of Europe. And no wonder: the passage from unmitigated servitude to unmitigated freedom (or, from the perspective of the administrators of the passage, from the extremes of regulation to the extremes of deregulation) happened there both unexpectedly and with tremendous haste, leaving no time for reflection and readjustment. The passage from one pole of the security–freedom axis to the other was compressed there into a matter of not much more than a decade. The most accurate image of the present state of Central–Eastern Europe is one of a landscape after the shock overlapping with a landscape after the vision of imminent consumerist orgy has been wiped out.

Leaving modernity

Carlo Bordoni   Leaving modernity is traumatic. It will continue to be for a long time because we are still aware of its resistance and conditioning wearing off.

We have come from modernity and find it very difficult to detach ourselves from it because it represents a source of certainty. Our *long goodbye* is slowed down by the natural tendency of every man to prefer what is certain to what is uncertain, the known to the unknown, to accept the pre-existing condition in its burdensome immutability. This is stability at the cost of dependence – because the primary cause of 'voluntary servitude', i.e. submission to power, even if it's not required – according to Étienne de la Boétie – is simply a *habit*.[5]

This is an attitude that is well represented by the insight of Walter Benjamin who, back in the 1930s, saw in the *Angelus Novus* (from a work by Paul Klee of 1910) the symbol of modernity: an angel flying away from a world in ruins and looking back at it as he flies.

Governments and politicians are of no help: they cannot show us which direction to take. They, themselves, do not understand; they are disoriented. They react in a contradictory way, sometimes pushing in preposterous directions, towards where they see a glimmer of certainty and the opportunity to recover the social control they have lost. The most consistent initiative is the attempt to use the global economy and finance to stabilize a situation of

unrest which they perceive as threatening, in order to bring it back
to a level of controllability, thus guiding the emergence of the new
and unknown on the tracks of what is already known and understood. It is like carrying out, as they put it, an operation to *reduce
complexity*. But any reduction, even if made with good intentions
to bring order and clarity, is always something forced, a betrayal
of the truth.

Every great crisis of transition – we can see this from past
history – has been terrible for those who experienced it: the other
possibility is to observe it in retrospect, when it is all over, and
make some sense of it, appreciating its positivity in relation to
future development, assessing its cultural significance, admiring
the intelligence of the men who were able to understand it and
nourish it.

Let's try to imagine, on the other hand, what the advent of
modernity must have been like for the people who lived in the
seventeenth and eighteenth centuries. Uprooted from their land
and forced to move to the edge of the industrial cities, which
spilled over chaotically into the desolate suburbs; forced into dark,
unhealthy hovels; reduced to working in factories that were real
prisons, with inhuman hours and wages that were insufficient to
feed a family. They were subjected to harassment, controls, economic and corporal punishment, treated like slaves, with no way
to escape from the system in which they found themselves trapped,
out of need and out of ignorance.

For them it was like living in an incomprehensible drama,
having to take a leap of faith, with moral and economic ruin facing
them in the threat of incipient mechanization. The uncertainty of
a future that no longer presented secure reference points; the
forced move from the countryside, and new rules of life, perceived
as unnatural, violent and inhuman. They experienced the despair
of watching the collapse of a world in which they had invested
their hopes for life, habits, desires and sense of fulfilment. It was
all erased by a crisis worse than a war, because, when a war ends,
the remnants of life are reconstructed on the basis of what existed
before, in an effort to get back to normality, to life before the war.
War is a momentary interruption, while every major transitory
crisis leads to a permanent change. Yet those men and women in
the seventeenth and the eighteenth centuries gave life to a more
solid, innovative, successful and unique period in human history,

which was bound to produce, in the centuries to follow, a great deal of change that would be identified by the term 'progress'.

To that period we gave the name of modernity, but for those who endured the upheaval at the time of its emergence, it was the end of a state of balance, of peace and happiness. Now we are in the same situation as those people, whose only hope lay in the destruction of the machines (for the Luddites) and in the re-establishment of the lost order – that is, in a return to a past they thought was better than the present. They too saw this upheaval as a difficult time to get through and they dealt with it with clenched teeth, paying with their blood and tears, as they waited for everything once again to be as it was before – if not for them, at least for their children.

But what they were experiencing was actually a real revolution, which led to lasting change, and was, as such, final. The perspectives were different; the choices, different; the rules of the game, different. That is because revolutions – within the traumatic upheaval that we are destined to face as well – have this devious side: they lend themselves beautifully to people who would change the rules to their own advantage. Agreements, promises, concessions, union agreements can all be revoked in the name of crisis; exceptional laws may limit libertarian guarantees that were previously taken for granted; interim measures may cancel overnight the economic certainties which whole generations believed in.

More than any other period in the past, modernity availed itself of foundations on which to build its certainties, because modernity fed on certainties and rules. What did the modernists want at the time of Hobbes, Locke and Spinoza? They demanded stability, legal certainty, recognition of private property and secure national borders, within which to thrive with the emergent industry and trade. Modernity made industrialization its primary objective, learning from the Renaissance the complexity of trade, through which to distribute and implement production.

Modernity has materialized and is materializing, based on quantity. It is desacralizing (faithful to its Enlightenment component) and would even have been anti-historical – since the Enlightenment abhorred history because it is the bearer of traditions and therefore of an irrational culture – if it had not been for nineteenth-century Romanticism, which recuperated the idea of history to justify and appraise the concept of the nation and its internal unity.

Its materialistic root remained solid for over three centuries, followed technological evolution and permeated into the frightening idea of progress, which is itself a quantitative idea; curiously, the idea of progress, as a constant drive, emerged at the same time as industrialization and the myth of perpetual motion. Progress is measured in the accumulation of production, wealth, consumption and knowledge. Above all, the good fortune and ability to produce income are its primary values, since the mercenary approach that ensured the Protestant Reformation of Luther and Calvin became established. The grace of God is recognized in success in business. However, this *liaison dangéreuse* between religion and power, useful for the success of bourgeois ethics, did not survive beyond the secular eighteenth century.

The teleological project of modernity transfers to the earth, and, with a clever *coup de théâtre*, promises instant happiness here, taking it away from religion, with its happiness that was promised in the afterlife, after death. Instead of bliss, of a spiritual happiness for eternity, in return for a hard-working, sin-free life, it proposes an immediate, material, quantifiable and expendable return for honest, hard-working, humble and thrifty conduct.

Such a balance worked perfectly, despite the social tensions, economic crises and subversive tendencies that tried to break up its foundations. No attempt at subversion, revolution, reform or trade union struggle ever undermined those foundations, that remained firmly in their place – beginning with the right to work. They held out until something began to crack on the inside.

There were many reasons for this and the crisis of modernity was triggered by the combination of several factors. First and foremost, by the contrast between conditions for the workers and for those in the ruling class, the bourgeoisie, which immediately experienced significant improvements on the path to progress supported by incontrovertible data, and also extended to the working class. In fact, even in the earliest historical–economic information documenting the progression of the industrial revolution, the living conditions of factory workers are described as being markedly improved: the workers own more clothes, wear shoes, and have increased the family income. It is just a shame that, compared to a life of poverty in the countryside, their quality of life gravely deteriorated: forced to work 14–16 hours a day in conditions of semi-slavery in order to feed themselves, forced to live in over-crowded, unhealthy slums, and forced to use women and children in the work force. A terrible existence, with the illusion of a better tomorrow, at least for their children.

But the promise of happiness on earth was never withdrawn. As progress advanced, it was gradually brought home to the mass of the population that industry was developing and the markets offered good earnings.

As for the foundations of modernity, the transformation of work in the post-World War period, progressive dematerialization and the consequent insecurity all played a key role in shaking them. Subsequently, globalization, which was needed by the multi-nationals as a quick fix for the problem of overproduction, entailed, as a sort of side-effect, the removal of borders and the emptying of social guarantees and democratic representation, in what has been called the *separation of power and politics*.

To this crisis of the foundations of modernity we can add the cultural aspect, connected to ideologies and to demassification, which has dealt a mortal blow to modernity.

According to Jean-François Lyotard, author of *The Postmodern Condition*, modernity ends its historic journey when its founda-tions or the *great narratives* crumble.[6] The structure of modernity, which developed from feudalism and was built on the innovations produced by the industrial revolution, is based on several *pillars*, amongst which ideology plays a leading role. It is the most impor-tant cultural foundation because it holds the essence of the modern: all that modernity represents in our eyes, rooted in the values of our time, in the belief in progress, in the almost dogmatic princi-ples of freedom and equality. Ideological belief has been our spir-itual leader for three centuries of history.

Ideology is the daughter of the Enlightenment. Introduced to consolidate ideas, it undermines a priori human behaviour and facilitates the interpretation of reality in an uncritical way. In 1796 the French philosopher Antoine-Louis-Claude Destutt de Tracy spoke of ideology as a scientific analysis of the faculty of thought, as opposed to metaphysics and psychology.[7] If man is what he thinks, in the Enlightenment vision of Destutt de Tracy, it is pos-sible to create a different society thanks to new ideas. Thus, ideol-ogy becomes a meta-science, the science of ideas, the science of all the sciences, but also a rigid pattern in which we can become trapped.

Stability is essential to ideology: it is its security, the key to an unambiguous interpretation of a true, immutable, perfect reality because it is opposed to all the unjust variants against which it fought and against which it constantly has to defend itself so as to avoid falling back into obscurantism. Stability implies immutability: ideology is *per se* conservative, since any change could undermine the stability and certainties gained.

Free from every codified reading, from every biased interpretation, ideology has guided and explained everything, from class struggle to authoritarianism. In its blind fury it has replaced the wars of religion and has become a 'justified' instrument of death, oppression, destruction and annihilation of man, all in the name of a presumed future benefit to the community, which, however, has often got lost on the way.

The worst crimes of modernity have been committed in the name of ideology: from the Stalinist purges to the Nazi concentration camps. In the 1950s, after the death of Stalin, there were those who still defended the ideological rigour and resoluteness of his political choices, in opposition to other, Western and capitalist, ideologies which were ready to take over.

Violence based on ideology is always justified, in that it may be necessary to defend a worse threat: Stalinism managed to last because there was a need to prevent any possibility of the return of Nazi–Fascism, of any resurgence of the extreme right. The same reasoning applies to those systems that have used all sorts of limitations of freedom, aggression and provocation of war in order to stem the communist threat.

In late modernity, ideology forcibly imposed a vision of the world, turning it into a dogmatic belief in which to trust, whose principles should not be called into question. Once fought against as a dangerous destabilizer of order, then adopted as a means of retaining power, ideology ends up being rejected because of its inability to uphold that order. It seems that the times have left it behind, that it has become an obsolete instrument to be put aside, since it can no longer be used profitably.

The crisis of modernity is really a *long goodbye*: it started in the second half of the twentieth century, and then went through postmodernity – an aesthetic phenomenon, rather than a philosophical and moral one – which burned itself out in a thirty-year period, but not without leaving a burdensome legacy. If, at first, postmodernism appeared as a desirable solution to the crisis of modernity, many observers, like you, have talked of the continuity of modernity, albeit in a degraded and *liquid* form, because of its uncertainty and inability to cling to stable points of reference. So, postmodernity, rather than being an evolution of modernity itself, lends itself to being considered instead as a sign of a profound ethical crisis, and modernity's attempt to overcome it without excessive effort.

Devoid of its solidity and its seemingly unshakable certainties, what remains of modernity is not at all appealing. Benjamin's *Angelus Novus* does not stop to linger over the ruins, but decisively flies away, even if his decision to leave that world grieves him.

Zygmunt Bauman   How do you know that we are leaving modernity? How would one know this anyway, assuming that things like them – beginnings or ends of eras – are at all knowable to insiders, people who live through it? The concept of an 'industrial revolution' was coined in the third quarter of the nineteenth century, well after it had started (as we now believe), and perhaps closer to its end than to its beginning. Hegel famously opined that the Owl of Minerva, the Goddess of Wisdom, spreads its wings at dusk: that is, at the end of the day, the night before another day, different from its predecessor. Saying that an era or an epoch is ending requires taking a vantage point in the future, when 'the end' will eventually happen, and looking back from there – as Klee/Benjamin's Angel of History did; but, first, we humans are not angels, and second, even the Angel drawn by Klee and analysed by Benjamin moved backwards, the point being that he could not see where he was moving to. This is one reason – but a crucial one – to question the validity of the (unjustly) common term 'late modernity'. How can we know that we live currently in late – instead of, for instance, early – modernity? We are allowed to use the denomination 'late antiquity' or 'late Middle Ages' only because both those eras ended a long time ago and the date of their death is (retrospectively, retrospectively!) fixed – even if somewhat arbitrarily; and let's note that those dates were picked quite a long time after the event. People present at the funeral of an era are as a rule unaware that they are in a graveyard or a crematorium. On the other hand, the history of public opinion is full to the brim not just with (false) announcements of new dawns and new ages, but also with (false) obituaries that are doomed to sink rapidly into oblivion. Remember 2012's world-wide expectation of the end of the world? We live in a time in which proclamations of ends and the impulse to add the prefix 'post' to the names of any part or aspect have become a common habit; if that, however, proves anything, it is the fairly widespread feeling that things are changing too fast to be grasped and that they resist being caught in flight – as well as that they are much more likely to vanish from view than to appear and settle there. Our culture is one of forgetting rather than of learning; and concerns with disposing of objects when they are no longer needed capture more attention than their production.

Reinhart Koselleck, the late historian of concepts, used the metaphor of a 'mountain pass' to characterize our present situation. We are climbing a steep slope trying to reach the peak. The slope is too steep to stop and camp, no construction would survive the crosswinds and rainstorms, so we have to go on climbing, and we do. But what is on the other side (if we ever get there to look at it), we cannot know till we reach the pass. It is a different metaphor, yet it conveys a situation strikingly similar to that of Klee/Benjamin's Angel of History.

The central message of the latter, as you surely remember, was that we know what we are running from, but have no inkling where to. Human imagination being what it is, that will not stop us from painting images of what is there in the future waiting for travellers to visit. But as long as we locate them in the future, we have no way of proving that they look the same as we painted them. When the moment to prove or refute the accuracy of our canvases arrives, the future will already have turned into a past. This is why history is a graveyard of unfulfilled hopes and frustrated expectations, while blueprints of paradise all too often turn out to be guidebooks to hell. As you've so rightly pointed out, 'the worst crimes of modernity have been committed in the name of ideology'.

But rather than bidding farewell to modernity, we are still waiting to gather the fruits of its promises and keep consoling ourselves that, this time over, they are really round the next corner

or the one after that. The promised fruits are comfort, convenience, safety, freedom from pain and suffering. From the start and
to this very day, modernity was about forcing nature to serve
obediently human needs, ambitions and desires – and about the
way of achieving that objective: more production and more consumption. We all, from the top to the bottom of society, tend to
panic whenever the sacrosanct 'economic growth' (the sole measure
we have been trained to use to evaluate levels of prosperity and
happiness – both societal and individual) falls to zero or – God
forbid! – below zero. Fascination with rising bliss and the instruments assuring/promising its rise is no less passionate than it was
100 or more years ago, and is still on the increase. The Church
of Economic Growth is one of the few congregations – perhaps
even the only one – that do not seem to lose the faithful and stand
a real chance of ecumenical status. The ideology of happiness-
through-consumption is the only one that stands a chance of
overriding, subduing and putting an end to all other ideologies. It
is no wonder that there was no shortage of sages interpreting its
global triumph as the end of the age of ideology or indeed the end
of history.

And don't let the presence of the usual number of dissenters,
apostates, heretics and renegades mislead us about the grip that
Church has on the bodies of the planet's inhabitants: the gospel
it teaches and promotes holds their minds as universally and com-
prehensively as no other 'grand narrative' ever managed. There is
no church without an institution of anathema and malediction,
and the number of the damned is a product of the church being
on the offensive rather than on the defensive, and is, as a rule,
taken for a sign of its strength rather than its weakness. Like most
churches, the Church of Economic Growth has also had its refor-
mations and counter-reformations, and divisions into denomina-
tions engaged in doctrinal disputes, but the differences between
them don't go as far as disagreeing on the sacrosanct object of
their cult. Nor does the game of musical chairs played by all political camps aspiring to a stint in governmental offices seem to affect
the gospel and the liturgy common to them all.

'A life without myth is itself the stuff of myth' – as John Gray
summed up human experience in the modern era.[8] The warning
signs accumulate, dear Carlo, indicating that the news of the
demise of 'grand narratives' was, as Mark Twain would say,

grossly exaggerated. A grand narrative dies only to be promptly replaced. Many of them however, are reincarnated rather than dying – or, relegated to the back pages of newspapers, they stay in a condition of suspended animation. As for the grandest of modern grand narratives – that of the progress in human control over Earth guided by the Holy Trinity of Economy, Science and Technology – it seems to be in better health than ever. Sigmund Freud wrote of illusions that 'just as they are unverifiable, they are also irrefutable'.[9] He explained: 'An illusion is not the same as an error, nor is it necessarily an error . . . In other words, we refer to a belief as an illusion when wish-fulfilment plays a prominent role in its motivation, and in the process we disregard its relationship to reality, just as the illusion itself dispenses with such accreditations.' The 'wish' in the illusion-generating 'wish-fulfilment' drive is much the same as it was throughout the duration of our modern age – the age of the intended/assumed/presumed human management of humans, nature, and their mutual interaction. Even geologists of our times call our era 'Anthropocene' – implying that the Holocene is now over and that it is now the human species that sets the tune and, willy-nilly, knowingly or not, by design or by default, decides the direction in which the planetary changes are about to move.

I'd say that one modern illusion which has been well and truly refuted is the illusion of achieving a human condition that is free from illusion.

Through postmodernity

Carlo Bordoni The postmodern period, on closer inspection, no longer exists. It is the name given to the short historical period between the 1970s and the end of the twentieth century, an overwhelming, chaotic period in which all the previous values and certainties of modernity were questioned.

Speaking of the postmodern today even seems to be an anachronism. Forty years ago, in the middle of the 1970s, it appeared to be the most innovative and original attempt to emerge from modernity unscathed, without losing its benefits. Enveloped in a glittering aura, it gave rise to enthusiasm and illusions, forced its way into art, orientated philosophy, revealed the fragility of ideologies and has laid bare the individual. Often misunderstood, misrepresented or misinterpreted, it spread to every aspect of contemporary life, and then went on to die a natural death with the advent of the third millennium. Because the postmodern, like all rites of passage, has served its purpose in ferrying us to a future as yet unnamed, leaving us with its uncertainties, its lack of values leaving an empty space waiting to be filled with new ethics; we are increasingly seduced by an intrusive and all-embracing technology, yet ever more and more alone.

Postmodernism was initially born in the United States as an innovative movement in architecture in the 1960s and 1970s, which was immediately recognized for its intolerance of environmental disharmony. It was on the very ruins of the apartment buildings of Pruitt-Igoe in St Louis (USA), a dilapidated complex whose demolition was completed on 15 July 1972, that the historian of architecture Charles Jencks (1977) ironically fixed the official date of the *death of modern architecture*.[10] The new sensibility found its most representative exponent in Robert Venturi, an architect who was opposed to the International Style of Le Corbusier and Mies van der Rohe, which was characterized by straight lines, rational, square, clean, but often cold and separated from reality of the urban fabric which contained them. Robert Venturi, Denise Scott Brown and Steven Izenour are the authors of *Learning from Las Vegas* (1972), in which they describe the qualities of postmodern architecture and propose the use of the iconic language of Pop Art, mixed with classical elements.[11] It is to Venturi that we owe the expression 'Less is a bore', closely linked with the motto of Ludwig Mies van der Rohe, 'Less is more.'

In advanced modernity, the postmodern architects have replaced the appealing forms of *aesthetic populism*, in which the distinctions between high culture and mass culture are eliminated. Where they can, they salvage details, embellishments, ornaments and quotations drawn from the past, in an imaginative construction of forms that sometimes comes close to kitsch and feeds off the cultural waste produced by consumption. The quotation (columns, ornaments) constitutes the historical link with the past, a period regarded in its entirety, to which they look with interest.

Postmodernism, starting with architecture, permeates all sectors of society, not just the cultural ones. In fact, social behaviour, the world of work, the economy and finance are all imbued with this innovative spirit, in an unexpected expansion, which contradicts the usual practice of a reverse movement, from the structure (the economy) to the superstructure (the culture). But, quite clearly, the unusual extension of the postmodern idea from the world of ideas to political and social practice is a sign of the times, in the innovative sense already predicted by the scholars of the Frankfurt School (Adorno, Horkheimer) after the end of World War II: the utopia of a critical theory that could change society.

From another point of view it can be seen, more easily, that the term 'postmodern', thanks to its ability to penetrate and suggest – and, for that matter, spread by the media – was immediately adopted in other fields and used (sometimes even inappropriately) to label a change in daily customs or practices. This was irrespective of the original meaning it had taken on in architecture, which denoted the new direction of critical thinking that was in opposition to French structuralism.

Unlike many thinkers who have made postmodernity the central theme of their studies, you have reached the conclusion that we still live within modernity, but it is a degraded modernity, in which everything has become unstable, precarious, temporary and uncertain. In an interview with Keith Tester, you acknowledge the difficulty in finding an appropriate definition to indicate the change taking place, first accepting the common sense of postmodernism and then abandoning it in favour of liquid modernity: 'My guess is that in the eighties I was not alone in desperately looking for a new cognitive frame into which our fast-changing image of the shared human world would fit better than it did in the one proffered by the "orthodox consensus". Postmodernism was . . . one possibility . . . to me, it seemed more appropriate than other "posts" available.'[12]

Yet much has changed in recent years. Modernity, as well as postmodernity, appears a long way off. It is not a question of nominalism, of attributing new unnecessary labels only for the sake of sensationalism, to attract the attention of the media, to create titles just for effect.

It is about recognizing a substantial change, a change that has occurred for a variety of historical and economic reasons, and which has radically changed the way of life that is called modernity. We will try to understand it, this momentous distinction between what is modern and what is not, but it presents itself as an aftermath: sometimes as a contradiction, other times as continuity, because history does not proceed in leaps ('natura non fecit saltum', said Darwin) but gradually, by small variations in register, which then turn out to be definitive.

We only notice these incessant movements (almost imperceptible adjustments as a result of events that seem random) at a distance, looking back, and are surprised and a little frightened at the great gap that has opened up between the way of life (and the way of thinking) then and that of today. It's true that the label of postmodernism is not a happy one. It contains in itself something negative, opposed to what was there before, but it is the most comprehensive attempt to show that something has changed. The new name was intended to explain that there had been a break with the past. It is all right, then, to call postmodernity that set of reactions to the already depleted modernity. That *post* placed before the substantive noun (because it was exactly that: a society based on stability) has been successful, has interpreted well what the observers of the 1970s meant.

That modernity was a closed affair, and that a new era opened up, whose characteristics were to be different, the lives of the people who lived in it were to be different. This was obvious. But the problem lies in something else. Postmodernism, just like all movements of immediate reaction to what preceded them, was of a temporary nature. It served to report an event in progress: a frenzied, even haphazard, series of adjustments – some as an enthusiastic and liberating reaction, others with the function of containment and rationalization. This was a heterogeneous blend that could only have a short life and would gradually peter out as society became aware of the change and adapted to the new conditions of life. So now postmodernism is over; it has completed its task of ferryman from modernity to the present, a present as yet unnamed. Sooner or later someone will invent the right definition for our time and will write it in the history books. Then postmodernism will be remembered in the same way as pre-romanticism or neo-classicism and we will notice that we have gone through postmodernity without even realizing it.

Postmodernity is the high point of the crisis of modernity and its attempt to overcome it. The ideologies which constituted the binding agent necessary for modernity, as did religion for the pre-industrial societies, cause, when they collapse, the loss of social cohesion. The bond of trust is broken between people who share the same ideals, who believe in common values, for which they fight and sacrifice themselves, feeling that the other is not a potential adversary, but a companion or colleague who pursues the same objectives. Solidarity among equals is based on this community of purpose and values, and when the ideals fail, it no longer has any reason to exist. On the contrary, he who, until recently, was considered a friend, now becomes a competitor, an adversary to watch out for, because he could deprive us of something, could snatch up the opportunity of a job, win the competition we had set our sights on, take advantage of a benefit reserved only to a few, or even just park his car in the only place available or, before our very eyes, grab the last bottle of wine on special offer on the supermarket counter.

Subjectivism is a cancer that eats away at modernity. It undermines and weakens its basis, preparing the ground for the liquefaction of society. Since the beginning of the twentieth century, there have been two main schools of thought that vie for supremacy: a rational current, that pursues the objectives of modernity and is objective in nature – that is, it looks at the social, at the collective. Whilst the different forms of this tendency share a common care and respect for the social, the current rationale is based on the Hegelian model and sees history as progress. This current of thought, that permeated the whole of the previous century, tends to maintain a dominant position, affecting cultural production, along with economic and professional relationships. In art and literature, for example, as realism argues, it could hardly be otherwise, given its 'rational' component, and it is ready to defend modernity even at the cost of suffering the inevitable disadvantages. It is positive and believes in social democracy and also in the current possibility of an improvement through struggle, commitment and mediation. It is, in short, a reformist current, but can be blown up into the ideological maximalism or even in revolution (as in the case of communism), without upsetting the pillars on which modernity rests, which it accompanies.

The other great trend is defined as irrationalist for its refusal to come to terms with modernity (or bourgeois society, if you will); of Kantian origin, it is highly critical of the social and aims at a re-evaluation of the single individual. For this reason, we speak of it as subjectivism. Its action unfolds in the wider appreciation of the subject, which becomes central and is able to determine the events through its will and its work. The subject, as the centre of human existence, is opposed to the mass that is devoid of self-determination. It goes without saying that such a position lends itself very well to endorsement by reactionary authoritarianism, which understands only the more immediate superficial aspects, and not the deep anti-modernist assumption (see Nietzsche's thought, usurped by Nazism) that is seen in a period of anti-authoritarianism and denial of any ideological imperative. The end of modernity sees the prevalence of the latter current and the weakening of the Hegelian model, with the inevitable consequence of a deep crisis that will result in postmodernism.

Postmodernity, with its exaltation of individualism, and its decline in the solidarity, respect for others and civilized behaviour that had marked the rise of the modern, ended up instead showing the face of a society that had regressed to the situation of the law of the survival of the fittest, the smartest, in which the most avid wins; there you lose the certainty of rights (you see campaigns, from time to time, opposing the judiciary and respect for justice), there the spirit of blind consumerism prevails without taking into account the resources of the planet (from water to energy), following the fierce instinct to have for oneself: a struggle for survival as if faced with the last chance of life (the absence of any future prospect) in which – just as for wild beasts – what is obtained by force or by cunning is taken home and consumed in loneliness.

This separation from the principle of civil society, which the community of values had guaranteed, thanks to the grand narratives that constituted the core of modernity, is accompanied by the uncontrollable need of the postmodern individual to gratify himself, develop and emerge from the anonymity forced on him first by massification and now by the loneliness of the global citizen. He does this in the only way possible, in the spirit of subjectivism, by exalting himself, showing off or selling himself in the market of public acceptance, as appropriate. This gives rise to the phenomenon of turning everything into a show, which has had a major impact in the media. The prevalence of the subject, regardless of his qualities and for the sole purpose of being recognized himself as an individual (*da-sein*, 'being-there', Heidegger would say), is an opportunity given to all equally, and fully exploited even when it is not called for. The important thing is to make their voices heard above those of others, to show off and attract attention, curiosity and interest, thus getting the 'visibility' needed to feel alive and to be able to spend on all public occasions. This is because being visible means existing: a condition that cannot be discharged alone and that calls for reflection in another person in order to be proven. Here lies the contradiction in terms of subjectivism: the prevalence of the individual needs, despite everything, a confrontation with society, recognition by others, otherwise it is meaningless.

But subjectivism also has a positive side, which consists in a return of the multitudes. At the time of the founding of the modern state, at the time of Hobbes, the multitudes were sacrificed on the altar of the community, and were repressed in the people, which has since become the official authorized and legitimate component of nations: a single body, sufficiently deprived of freedom to make into modern citizens. The multitudes that emerged then from feudalism and were not considered sufficiently reliable for the new social construction of the nation-state now have a historic opportunity to redeem themselves and play their hands. They are the ones to enjoy the historic turning point represented by postmodernism, precisely because of the prevalence of subjectivism, but they are also the first to endure heavy pressure for the re-establishment of social control in other forms.

Because it is clear, as it was for Hobbes and other builders of the modern state in the seventeenth century, that the multitudes – by their very nature – are difficult to control. They manage to avoid any restriction, any conditioning that they would not be prepared to accept peacefully – a little like web surfers, who greatly resemble the multitudes.

Today we seek new ways of social control, since it is no longer possible to rely on ideology and the work ethic (both outmoded according to public opinion). And in order to obtain control, it is necessary to carry out a re-foundation of the social system, resetting all the options, concessions and privileges acquired during the last decades of modernity, when it had to come to terms with the community to maintain its power.

For this reason, we have to start again from the beginning: from social differences. Put everyone in his place, and then we'll see. The economic crisis, so conveniently operated and driven by the markets, by financial groups, by the needs of a globalized economy, faces the task of restoring social control, which the crisis of modernity lost sight of.

Zygmunt Bauman You classify the decade or two during which postmodernist fashions in arts, through mimicry or shifts in mental attitude, spilt over into ever wider areas of human thought and practices, as a 'rite of passage'. You have a point here. Victor Turner, who elaborated that term borrowed from Arnold van Gennep's 1909 study with the same title, argued that there is no direct, instant passage from one form of life or one socially defined identity to the next; when one form or identity in the socially set life itinerary follows another, the two are, as a rule – and perhaps must be for the passage to become recognized and acknowledged – separated from each other by an intermediary, 'between and betwixt' period of, so to speak, 'social nakedness', in which individuals are stripped of the paraphernalia of their previous, now abandoned role and status before they are allocated, supplied with and don the new paraphernalia ascribed to the status and role they are about to assume and play. Using the 'rites of passage' in the individual life-story as an allegory, we may visualize the interval between two distinct social arrangements as a time of dismantling the old material and mental structures before the new structures are designed, put together and in place. Personally, I prefer to call that 'between and betwixt' period in socio-political history an 'interregnum' (in a form recently updated by Keith Tester, that concept denotes a time when the old ways of having things done no longer work properly, but new and more effective ways have not yet been made available).

The trouble, though, with both concepts – the 'rite of passage' when applied to social history, instead of to the socially fixed sequence of an individual journey through life, as much as with 'interregnum' – is that, when viewed from inside, things and their relations are continually *in statu nascendi*: it is not known where they are heading or what the dismantled and melted structures will eventually be replaced with. When we think of a 'passage', we have in mind a stretch of road or a time-span leading from a 'here' to a 'there'. As you know, however, for 'postmodernists', a 'there' was as much unknown as it was deemed irrelevant and unworthy of serious concern. By and large, most, if not all, the

concerns of postmodernist artists were focused on the 'dismantling', 'deconstructing', and, all in all, destructing jobs. And it was
not at all insignificant that the postmodernist movement started
from architecture, the area of human activity from which the very
idea of 'order' (*ordo*) was drawn at the threshold of the modern
era to be metaphorically applied to the totality of human activity
in the world, including society, now considered the most remark-
able among human constructions. The 'postmodern' architects
described and analysed by Charles Jencks assaulted the very arche-
type of 'order' inherited from Vitruvius when his ancient tract *De
architectura* was re-discovered by builders in fifteenth-century
Europe, and so also, by proxy, its derivatives, such as system-ness,
harmony, structure, pattern, fit.

This seems to be – at the moment of my writing, at any rate
– a relatively lasting sediment of the postmodernist episode: the
mistrust of all and any order, synchronic and diachronic alike;
questioning of the idea of 'order' as such; the tendency to raise
'flexibility' and 'innovation' above 'stability' and 'continuity' in
the hierarchy of values; melting with no moulds prepared in which
to pour the molten metal. All this suggests the prospect of the
present interregnum lasting for a rather long time. And let's
remember that one of the most prominent traits of a period of
interregnum is that anything, or almost anything, can happen,
though nothing, or almost nothing, can be done with any degree
of confidence and self-assurance.

Folk wisdom counsels resisting the counting of chickens before
they are hatched, while the great Russian poet Vladimir Mayakowski, drawing on his own rather dramatic series of experiences
during another 'interregnum period' stretching from the fall of the
tsarist regime to the emergence of Stalin's totalitarian state, warned
his contemporaries not to paint epic canvases in a time of revolutions because they would surely be torn apart. When ignoring his
advice, we are keen to repeat the mistake of patching up imagined
structures out of fleeting fashions, 'totalities' out of episodes,
trends out of diffuse and uncoordinated moves – and recycling
current talks of the town into hastily concocted sociological theories. All the same, it is worth remembering that the phrase sports
commentators love to use, 'you are witnessing history in the
making', leaves unanswered the questions of a possible hiatus
between what is there to be witnessed and what the witnesses

believe they are witnessing, and of how much staying power a historiography written by eyewitnesses is entitled to boast.

Personally, as you may know, I felt uneasy when, for the lack of a better term, I had to use the label of 'postmodernity' to denote a change in the socio-cultural setting which called for revised or brand-new analytical tools to be grasped, comprehended and described. I felt uneasy mainly on two accounts.

First, whatever the meaning intended by its user, this term implied that we were already beyond the modern era, which was evidently untrue. As François Lyotard wittily – though still very seriously and correctly – observed, one needs first to be postmodern in order to become modern. The arrival of what was misleadingly called '*post*-modernity' was an internal event inside the history of the modern era, which was still far from surmising as much as the titles of its forthcoming chapters, let alone the placement of its finishing line. If anything, that event laid bare the essential features of the modern way of being-in-the-world of which the 'pre-postmodern' modernity was blissfully unaware (this was, as I understand it, the intended meaning of Lyotard's paradox). The so-called 'postmodernity' was the time for learning which of the promises of modernity were fraudulent or naive pretensions, which of its ambitions were manifestations of condemnable hubris, and which latent intentions were covered up by loudly declared objectives. One could say, deploying Hegelian terminology, that 'postmodernity' was a crucial stage on the long and tortuous road from 'modernity in itself' to 'modernity for itself' – aware of its own abilities and its limitations, or at least postulating the need for such awareness and coming somewhat closer to acquiring it. The term 'postmodernity' masked and disguised rather than revealed the true sense of what was happening at the time.

The second reason to feel uneasy was the purely negative content suggested by the term. It implied (wrongly, as I tried to point out) what the present realities no longer are, but gave very little – if any – information about their own defining attributes; it called for an inventory of things rejected and left behind, rather than for a reasoned catalogue of things that took their place. I felt therefore the need to coin and deploy a term aimed at expressing what those new realities (or at least their most distinctive traits) are, instead of focusing on what they are not, and so what is it that justified readjustment of the extant sociological tools. From this came the choice of the metaphor of 'liquidity'. It is true that modernity from its very start was busy 'melting all solids', but it did not do it because of some inbuilt dislike or resentment of solidity, but because it found the extant 'solids' not solid enough – indeed, in a state of advanced putrefaction. The original intention – at least, the originally declared intention – was to replace the seedy, dilapidated solids that were losing their holding power with solids designed and forged in the works of reason and thus resistant to erosion and deformation (an idea which finds its fullest expression, again after the manner of the Owl of Minerva, in Talcott Parsons' much later model of a 'self-equilibrating system' – a state of affairs able to return promptly to its steady form thanks to its own homeostatic contraptions, whenever it is pushed or veers off course). This is, however, no longer the case. Before the molten stuff had time to petrify into a stable, solid form, it had melted again. Our settlements are temporary, transient, supplied with the clause 'until further notice'. The 'structures' we zealously concoct in our self-defeating drive towards 'order' are, so to speak, 'biodegradable' – they start decomposing the moment their composition has been completed, or, all too often, even before it has been. We do not trust them to stay fit for long in kaleidoscopically changing circumstances. It is not the quality of solidity which we require of the interim-settlement, temporary-arrangement or emergency-measure-style structures we compose, but the quality of flexibility. The knots we tie need to be amenable to untying with one pull of the string – something akin to our new ability to bring in or remove an image on the iPad screen with one finger.

However, as Richard Sennett pointed out, 'perfectly viable businesses are gutted or abandoned, capable employees are set adrift rather than awarded, simply because the organization must prove to the market that it is capable of change'[13] – and he commented: 'Revulsion against bureaucratic routine and pursuit of flexibility has produced new structures of power and control, rather than created the conditions which set us free'.[14] As I have argued elsewhere, flexibility, the trademark of liquid modernity, an asset for the rulers and the handicap of the ruled, is indeed the new strategy of domination.[15] Rather than normative regulation, panopticon-style surveillance and policing, it is now superiors' capacity for Houdini-like vanishing acts that holds their subordinates in the condition of servitude and impotence. The other face of this flexibility for some is fixation and immobilization for some (in fact, many more) others. Mobility is the principal stratifying factor in liquid-modern society. Besides, 'No long term', the precept of liquid-modern reason and the pivot guiding liquid-modern rationality, is – to quote Sennett once more – a 'principle which corrodes trust, loyalty and mutual commitment'[16] – with devastating consequences for the character of human ethical consciousness and solidarity.

Yet, all those crucial, indeed defining, traits of our early 21st-century reality, which the concept of 'liquid modernity' cannot but move into the centre of attention, had been either totally omitted from consideration or relegated to the background by the concept of 'postmodernity'.

Deconstruction and denial

Carlo Bordoni   A period of transition like postmodernism tries to find confirmation in philosophical consideration of the need to transform the past, whose instruments of understanding reality appear outdated and insufficient. This new way of thinking is well represented by the deconstructionism of Jacques Derrida and by the weak thought of Gianni Vattimo and Pier Aldo Rovatti, who are deeply influenced by both Nietzsche and Heidegger. Vattimo underlines the essence of what is not foundational to postmodernism, drawing inspiration from Heidegger, and for him *thinking is remembrance, regain–accept–distort*, i.e. turning to look at modernity and its foundations with detachment, as if looking at memorials that represent our past.[17] They constitute a discrete image of a people that lived before us and of whom there are now only traces (texts). The postmodern observer stands on the other side of those events (for this *is* 'post') and is therefore outside history.

Derrida's deconstructionism is perfectly suited to representing the postmodern vision, through a strict process of negation of the modern spirit, which does not correspond to an equally positive fresco of the new. Deconstructionism is really the functional philosophy of postmodernism: self-referential, provocative, intuitive, obscure, cryptic, creative, fiercely critical, it is the last link in a chain that has its roots in the irrationalism of Nietzsche. It shows a close relationship with the thought of Heidegger, champion of twentieth-century subjectivism, which reflects a dangerous affinity with Nazism, of which he was, for a certain period of time, an eager supporter. While the Hegelian philosophy and its progenies, including Marxism, ride modernity and support its values and objectives (history, progress, the collective), irrationalism fights against it and exposes its contradictions (Nietzsche). It puts the spotlight back on the individual, on the subject that makes sense of the world around him (Husserl); it denies history and progress, pointing out the exceptional nature of the individual (Heidegger), who has the task of interpreting the world. This concept was of great importance in the long process of serving a default notice on modernity, while Derrida, the philosopher who, more than any other, was able to connect Heidegger's embryonic concept of *Destruktion* to postmodernity, *deconstructs* the certainties of modernity and exposes its illusory and biased nature. He did it using the weapons of philosophy, without entering into the political (even during 1968 he preferred to remain on the sidelines) and social issues.

However, sociology, the science of interpretation of facts and social changes – which is better prepared for this task, and is also used to supporting modernity with its falsely objective instruments, according to the original needs of *Wertfreiheit* (Ethical Neutrality), developed by one of its most influential founding fathers, Max Weber – found itself in crisis in those years.[18] Now far from the warnings delivered by the Frankfurt School, whose only remaining member is philosopher Jürgen Habermas, the sociology of crisis used negative descriptions of a changing society for a long time, and finds in you, Zygmunt, its wisest and most explicit exponent.

An understanding of the changing world, which is leaving behind centuries of reassuring solidity, finds an effective metaphor of postmodernity in the concept of liquid society, where everything is mobile, uncertain, temporary. The social change you describe tends to build a flexible sociological model, which serves more to understand and explain than to criticize. Such a task is more than ever praiseworthy, almost redeeming, in times of general confusion and uncertainty about the objectives to pursue.

The individual who has lived through postmodernity, has been subjected to the collapse of ideologies, has lost his reference values, job security and ethical code, hit by unparalleled economic and existential uncertainty, can now find in your *comprehensive* sociology reasons for reassurance and peace. In fact, the sociology of postmodernity is quick to produce large comprehensive essays on the change observed, focusing largely on the examination of individualism, loss of social solidarity and globalization, as if it were dealing with a phenomenon already under way.

On the interpretation of postmodernism there is a documented contrast between Lyotard and Habermas, who has repeatedly expressed his opposing view, detailing it especially in *The Philosophical Discourse of Modernity*.[19] While, for Lyotard, postmodernism produces a liberation from the ideology of capitalism and imperialism, for Habermas the end of the great narratives is a disaster. Indeed, for him postmodernism emerges in oppostion to modernity, as a negation, and therefore does not have its own autonomy, it is just a *sign of the times*, derived from the impasse in which we currently find Enlightenment thought, which identifies itself with modernity. In short, modernity is not over: indeed, it must be nurtured so as to avoid returning to obscurantism.

The extension of postmodernism to every sector of society, with inroads even into personal and sentimental relationships, contributed, however, to confusion and made postmodernism into a sort of negative *blanket term* to use with excessive levity, when trying to give an explanation for the great changes that characterize our time. Its negative character, which is therefore oppositional to a mode of being and evaluating, as well as a precise ethic that recognizes itself in modernity, means that many observers reject the idea of postmodernism, just as you do (in agreement with Habermas on this), preferring to consider the present as an internal modification to modernity itself, which you define as *liquid*.[20]

But whether one accepts the concept of postmodernism as a break with a practically unsalvageable past, or whether you prefer to speak of a 'liquefaction' that slipped into modern times, it seems clear, however, that it is still an occasional *condition* and therefore intended to be *temporary*. A condition endured rather than desired, with all the characteristics of a crisis of transition, one of the great historic crises of transition referred to by the Americans as a 'Great Divide'. A large structural division, which therefore has significant consequences for culture, human relations, the destiny of the world in which we live, and separates the known past from a future full of unknowns. The Great Divides are cathartic moments from which there is no turning back; they are decisive steps for humanity that, once made, allow no second thoughts, no going back, and only after many years do we realize the shocking extent of the definitive change they brought about. We have no information about many great divisions in the history of man: the greatest was the introduction of writing, a revolutionary technology that changed the human brain and laid the foundation for cumulative knowledge.

But postmodernism has gone. Its life cycle has come to an end, its role as ferryman finished. It has left us on an unknown and treacherous shore, facing the daunting prospect of new threats and an economic crisis of global proportions which is difficult to understand, because the new world we have set foot on, which followed on from modernity and postmodernity, conceals dark intentions. It is the task of sociology, in the new sense you indicated, not just to confine itself to observing the facts without judging them, but to get to the bottom of the reasons for their occurrence: to understand and help us to understand the present to prepare for tomorrow. It is the only way left to us to alleviate uncertainty.

Postmodernity is a transition between modernity and the new stage that does not yet have a name, though its essential features are already beginning to take shape. All stages of transition – such as Pre-romanticism at the beginning of the nineteenth century or Decadentism before the twentieth century – suffer from serious problems of adjustment, of painful regret for things lost, and are characterized by extreme emotionalism, a breaking with the past, the search for a new equilibrium. But, unlike other major crises of the past, postmodernism was not the bearer of great innovations in a positive sense, apart from the start of the great movement of demassification which is still in progress. So, when did it start? Possibly the end of the 1970s. By common agreement, the symbolic date is 1979, the year of publication of the emblematic work by Lyotard, which suggests that the classification of the postmodern phenomenon was essentially European, before being extended to the whole Western world. More broadly speaking, it can be said to have begun with the energy and oil crises of the 1970s, an irreparable rift caused by a period which experienced economic prosperity and the development of generalized consumerism (the 1960s).

The end of modernity lies here, in the students and workers' revolts, the cultural revolution imported from Mao's China, and the first disappointment of a wealthy consumer society. Since then, nothing has been the same. Even the media – the most important being television – are losing their unique authority and supreme ability to obtain agreement, contributing to the *ideological* massification which had already begun with radio and the cinema under Fascism, Nazism and other totalitarian systems all over the world. It is the collapse of a world that can no longer keep up with the times. The new, still timid, technologies, miniaturization, the opening-up of radio and television frequencies, lend themselves to undermining the foundations of thought and produce a unique exchange of ideas: a movement of innovation – alternative, they said – whose protagonists are the young people.

However, it was destined to be a short tumultuous period, marked by dark and violent attempts to return to order: attempts at restoration, coups, secret plots, attacks – the 'years of lead' (the period of political turmoil in Italy, the 1970s to the early 1980s) – which were followed by the extremism of opposing factions (the kidnapping of Aldo Moro, the Rote Armee Fraktion, the Red Brigade), equally bound to have deleterious effects and, despite self-nomination and self-glorification, of a clearly reactionary nature. The common features both shared, even if they were unaware of it, were opposition to the change under way, a failure to understand the gravity of the crisis, clumsy attempts to direct it towards improbable objectives. How long did all this last? Postmodernism spanned thirty years, until the beginning of the twenty-first century, with some persistent fringes and a few inevitable regurgitations which lead us to feel that it still exists today, while it is clear that it is definitively over, so much so that its most dominant features now seem distant to us and no longer viable. If we wanted to give a date – a striking symbol, to define better the end of postmodernism – we could take 11 September 2001, the date of the attack on the Twin Towers in New York, a tragic event – broadcast live on TV around the world: a painful ending to a period, which has spread by being turned into a spectacle. Another symbolic limitation to report, even if a less dramatic one, could be the death of Jacques Derrida (2004), the most significant philosopher of postmodernity (it is no coincidence that he too is French, like Lyotard).

Now postmodernism is behind us: we see it like a ghostly succession of fireworks in the night of dying modernity. Like the result of a biological drive to survive and celebrate before everything is finished, before the serious problems of *later* begin, of which neither the extent nor the face is known, but the consequences are feared. A time that is anything but negative, on closer inspection, despite the fact that its definition suggests that it is something in opposition to the past: a denial of modernity, of what we no longer are.

To try to understand where we are going, it is wise to analyse what postmodernity – or whatever you want to call it – represented for us, the inhabitants of the twenty-first century, and what its recognizable features were. In the first place, there was individualism. Postmodernism is the great ferryman that, in conjunction with the end of the millennium, leads us out of two centuries in the name of the collective, the social. The big push began with Hegelianism in the nineteenth century and continued with Marx, the class struggle, and then mass society, then ending up in the doldrums of demassification around the 1970s and 1980s. It is no coincidence that 1989 is the year of the fall of the Berlin wall, a liberating event that preceded the fall of the Soviet regime, or the sinking of the great communist illusion – that is, a collectivist one, of a society that can provide for everyone according to his needs. This was replaced by a widespread and aggressive individualism whereby everyone looks out for himself, at the expense of others and without worrying about the good of society.

The world that leaves postmodernism behind is a world that has become too limiting for the individual, an oppressive and intrusive world, where the individual is unable to assert himself because of the excess of bonds that hold him duty-bound to others: excellence cannot emerge, at the expense of quality.

Industries want to be able to hire on the basis of merit and not according to the unemployment register, just as they want to fire absentees or those who are not productive. Contrary to what happened in previous years, in which there was a strong sense of social solidarity supported by a powerful union, the idea of a liberalization of the labour market is becoming more accepted by public opinion, culminating in the regularization of short-term contract work, and temporary or fixed-term employment. The official legalized start (not the cultural one, which had already happened) of precariousness in employment. A new era opens up. The disintegration of the mass, united by a careful conditioning induced by the media and then by rampant consumerism (which for some time had been the symbol of happiness), produced striking effects: people who suddenly felt isolated, detached from a recognizable community context, single or in nuclear couples, at first unable to communicate and understand the unusual situation they were experiencing. Deprived of values to refer to – in the meantime, the effects of the crisis of ideologies are making themselves felt – their economic and existential security is threatened, and they are therefore unwilling to help others. They are concerned only with their own personal interests and with protecting themselves in the face of an unstable present and an uncertain future. The world is fluid, an agitated ocean in which economic, social and cultural relations combine incessantly. Great movements, powerful upheavals and exhausting undertows that give an idea of the extreme instability typical of large systems on a global level.

Inside this huge liquid world move billions of lives, often overwhelmed and disorientated by the liquidity of the environment in which they live. Pushed into random directions against their will and with limited opportunities not only to determine their own future, but also to understand the reasons for what is happening. Lives immersed in the liquidity of life – perhaps submerged. Because there is no trace of their lives, their work, or their actions on the taut and compact surface of the ocean-world. Beneath the surface, a *hidden society* forms that adapts on a daily basis to the conditions of a changing environment. Just like the algae in the sea that tenaciously resist by clinging to the sand and then let themselves go in the motion of the waves. If the thrust of the waves is too strong, they are uprooted and carried away, but they are ready to cling immediately elsewhere, stretching their vital ganglions towards the first available anchorage they can latch on to.

This hidden society is made up of multitudes, and based on adaptability to adverse conditions. Its existence is a continuous resistance to increases and decreases, to exceptional events, to natural and moral disasters, to broken promises, to the regulations that amend certainties which seem to be acquired, to collapses, to sudden shutdowns, to foreclosures, to marginalizations, discriminations, to frustrated expectations, to restrictive interpretations, to projects that *are not covered in our programmes*, to scams, to serious crimes, to unpaid compensation, to mishaps, to malfunctions, to disappointments.

This submerged society is made up of ordinary people who are emerging from the mass society and its adamantine certainties, and who no longer have fixed reference points; people who think they live a normal life and discover, not without embarrassment, that they have lived in postmodernity without knowing it. And then, at the very moment in which they become aware (not without confusion and with strong reservations), they hear that postmodernism is also a thing of the past.

Today is a book without a title and, at least for the time being, without a label of convenience, applied so as to shake off the fear of the unknown.

It is not expected that ordinary people will know what modern, postmodern or suchlike means; however, it is necessary to the next level, that of the surface of the liquid world. For those who live immersed in the liquidity, specialist terminology is a pointless exercise: it makes little sense and is not accountable for, at least not theoretically, the problems they encounter. The daily experience with which it is necessary to confront ourselves in the immediate future is represented by the increase in the cost of petrol, bills, consumer products, taxes, the lack of jobs for our children, and the difficulty in paying our mortgages. It does not matter whether or not it is a consequence of postmodernity or just one of many moments of crisis. The important thing is to resist.

Perhaps Jean-François Lyotard was right when he said that modernity ends with the absurdity of the concentration camps, the most tragic example of a totalizing institution that goes beyond the limits of what is human and therefore cannot produce anything worse in the escalation of horror and of abuse of the individual.

Zygmunt Bauman   Our fathers could quarrel about what needs to be done, but they all agreed that once the task had been defined, the agency would be there, waiting to perform it – namely, the states armed simultaneously with power (ability to get things done) and politics (the ability to see to it that the right things are done). Our times, however, are striking for the gathering evidence that agencies of this kind are no longer in existence, and most certainly not to be found in their previous usual places. Power and politics live and move in separation from each other and their divorce lurks around the corner. On the one hand, we see power safely roaming the no-man's-land of global expanses, free from political control and at liberty to select its own targets; on the other, there is politics squeezed/robbed of all or nearly all of its power, muscles and teeth. We all, individuals-by-decree-of-fate, seem to be abandoned to our own individual resources, sorely inadequate for the grandiose tasks we already face, and the even more awesome tasks to which we suspect we will be exposed unless a way of avoiding them is found. At the bottom of all the crises in which our times abound lies – as we have indicated briefly before – the crisis of *agencies* and *instruments of effective action* – and its derivative: the vexing, demeaning and infuriating feeling of having been sentenced to *loneliness* in the face of *shared* dangers.

We also mentioned the widely popular response to that crisis of agency, often called 'movement of the indignant'. But what is it that 'the indignant' are indignant of? If they leave their CCTV-protected homes to gather on and 'occupy' public squares, they do it to express their indignation at the indolence of extant political institutions supposed to represent their interests and to recycle them into action, and so also at their own impotence. They hope (whether realistically, or in vain, remains to be seen) to find out on the crowded squares what they could not in their gated communities.

One way or the other, indignation is there, and a precedent has been set for unloading it: through going to the streets and occupying them. The recruiting pool for potential occupiers is enormous, and growing day by day. Having lost faith in a salvation coming from 'on high' as we know it (that is, from parliaments and governmental offices) and looking for alternative ways of getting the right things done, people are taking to the streets on a voyage of discovery and/or experimentation. They transform city squares into open-air laboratories, in which tools of political action hoped to match the enormity of the challenge are designed or come across by chance, put to the test, perhaps even pass a baptism of fire. And for a number of reasons city streets are good locations for such laboratories, and for quite a few other reasons the laboratories set there seem to deliver, if only for the time being, what has been sought elsewhere in vain.

The 'people in the streets' phenomenon has shown thus far its ability to remove some of the most hated objects of people's indignation, the figures blamed for their misery – like Ben-Ali, Mubarak or Gaddafi. It still needs to prove though that, however effective its prowess has been in clearing the building site, it can also be of use in the building job that comes after. The second, no less crucial, unknown is whether the site-clearing operation may be accomplished as easily in other than dictatorial countries: tyrants tremble at the very sight of people taking, un-commanded and uninvited, to the streets – but, globally, leaders of democratic countries, and the institutions they put together to guard the perpetual 'reproduction of the same,' seem thus far not to have noticed and not be worried; they go on re-capitalizing the banks scattered over the countless Wall-Streets of the globe, whether they are occupied by indignant locals or not. As Hervé le Tellier wittily observed, our leaders speak of 'political scandal, barbaric chaos, catastrophic anarchy, apocalyptic tragedy, hysterical hypocrisy' (using all along, let us note, terms coined by our joint Greek ancestors more than two millennia ago!), implying that the blunders and misdemeanours of one country and its government could be blamed for the crisis into which the whole European system has fallen – and, by the same token, exonerating the system itself.

And yet there is an even graver issue to address: 'people occupying streets' may well shake the very foundations of a tyrannical or authoritarian regime aspiring to full and continuous control over the subjects' conduct, and above all expropriating them of the right to initiative. This, however, hardly applies to a democracy that without a major shake-up may easily take huge doses of discontent in its stride and assimilate any amount of opposition. The Movimientos de los indignados in Madrid, Athens or New York, unlike their predecessors – for instance, people occupying Václavské Náměstí in communist Prague – are still waiting in vain for their presence in the streets to be noticed by their governments, let alone to influence, however minimally, their policies. This applies offline – to people in the streets. It also applies, to a much greater degree, online: people on Facebook, Twitter, Myspace trying earnestly to change history, including their own biography, with blogging, spurting venom, blowing trumpets, twittering and calling into action.

Another issue is that of the quality of political leaders, and indeed of political leadership itself, which you've so poignantly analysed. Allow me to quote in this context a note I sent to *Sociologicky Casopis*, a Czech sociological journal, in which I tried to assess the meaning of Václav Havel's recent departure:

A few days ago hundreds of thousands, perhaps more than a million people took to the streets and public squares of Prague to bid farewell to Václav Havel, according to many observers the last great political-cum-spiritual leader (spiritual, in great measure, thanks to his political greatness – and political, in great measure, thanks to his spiritual greatness), the likes of whom we are unlikely to witness again in our life-time. What we are unlikely to witness either are comparable numbers of people prompted to take to the streets by their gratitude to and respect for a statesman, rather than by their wholesale indignation, resentment and derision for people in power and the politics 'as we know it.' In their farewell to Havel, the mourners bewailed a political leader who in sharp distinction from the political operators of today gave power to the powerless, instead of stripping them of whatever shreds of power they might have retained.

Havel was one of those few – ever fewer and further between – political/spiritual leaders who single-handedly challenged, and to an enormous effect, the irony and derision with which the capacity of an individual to change the course of events has been all too often treated by the learned as much as by popular opinion. Future historians would most probably place the name of Václav Havel on the list of great individuals who 'made a difference' – without whom the world would not and could not be like the world we've inherited. Historians would perhaps confirm as well the fearful anticipations of millions of mourners who felt bereaved by Havel's departure, adding to that name the designation of 'the last in line of the great political leaders who shaped the world we inhabit'. Bidding farewell to Havel, most of us – including our present-day appointed/elected leaders (however reluctant they may be to admit it) – have all the right and all the duty to look at themselves as dwarfs sitting on the shoulders of giants, of whom Václav Havel was, undoubtedly, one of the greatest. We look around in vain for those giants' successors – and we do it in a time when we need them even more than ever before in our collective memory.

Havel left us at a time when people at the head of state governments, even the governments of the so-called 'powerful states', are looked upon with a steadily rising dose of irony and disbelief. The trust in the ability of the extant political institutions to influence the course of history, let alone to control it or change it if required, is dwindling. The trust in politics as such has been set afloat by the repeated sightings of the government's impotence – and thus far seeks in vain a safe haven fit for mooring and casting an anchor. It is ever clearer that the inherited network of political institutions can no longer deliver, whereas a new toolbox for effective collective action is, at the utmost, at a design stage, unlikely to be put into production soon or even recognized as worthy of being produced.

The growing weakness of the extant executive powers, which is ever more likely to be incurable, has been long noted. It is too blatantly displayed to be overlooked. Heads of the most powerful governments meet on Friday to debate and draw the right line of action to take, only to wait, trembling, till the stock exchanges reopen on Monday to find out whether their decision has a leg to stand on. Indeed, the present state of interregnum is not of a recent birth, not very recent at any rate. Its ever more obtrusive presence was not just signalled, but recognized and reflected, years ago, in the growing deficit of trust in the established vehicles of collective action, in falling interest in institutionalized politics and in the relentlessly spreading – and already widespread, indeed ambient – sentiment that salvation, if it was at all conceivable, would not and/or could not arrive from on high. We may add that the drivers and conductors of the above-mentioned vehicles, whether acting singly or severally, have for a long time been doing everything imaginable to set that trust afloat by denying and discrediting the merits of acting in common, and to keep trust un-anchored – by admonishing, nagging and nudging men and women, far and wide, into believing that, even if they are suffered in common, their shared problems have nevertheless thoroughly individual causes, and therefore can and should be individually faced and tackled, and individually, through the use of individual means, resolved.

With ever-more-evident social divisions seeking in vain a political structure in which they could reflect themselves as well as political tools capable of servicing that reflection, the paramount, well-nigh defining trait of the state of 'interregnum' (namely, its tendency to allow almost anything to happen, yet nothing to be accomplished with any degree of self-assurance and certainty of results) may well manifest itself with a still unprecedented force and even greater consequences.

This is what was to be expected in our times, dubbed in advance an 'interregnum' by Antonio Gramsci (a term which had sunk unduly into oblivion, and for much too long, but fortunately excavated recently and dusted-off thanks to Professor Keith Tester): times at which the evidence piles up almost daily that the old, familiar and tested ways of doing things no longer work, while their more efficient replacements are nowhere in sight – or too precocious, volatile and inchoate to be noticed, or to be taken seriously when (if) noted.

We may safely assume that people who, in rising numbers, take nowadays to the streets and settle for weeks or months on end in the improvised shelters pitched on public squares, know – or, if they don't actually know, certainly have enough opportunity to guess or suspect – where they are running *from*. They know for sure, or at least they have good reasons to believe that they know, what they would *not* like to go on being done. What they don't know, though, is what needs to be done *instead*. Even more importantly, they have no inkling *who* could prove to be potent and willing enough to do whatever they believe is the right step to take. Twitter and Facebook messages summon them and send them to public squares to protest against 'what is' – the message-senders, however, keep mum on the moot question of what kind of 'ought' that 'is' shall be replaced with; or they portray an 'ought' in sufficiently broad, sketchy, vague and above all 'flexible' outlines to pre-empt any part of it ossifying into a bone of contention. They also keep prudently silent about the thorny issue of the compatibility or incompatibility of their demands. Tweeters and Facebook message-senders can neglect such caution only at the peril of the cause they promote. Were they to disregard the iron rules of all effective digital calling-to-arms, and all successful from-online-to-offline strategy, they would risk their messages being stillborn or dying without issue: few if any tents would be pitched on public squares in response to their calls, and very few would be holding their initial residents in them for long.

Building sites, it seems, are nowadays in the process of being collectively cleared in anticipation of a different management of

State of Crisis

space. People on the move do that job, or at least earnestly try to. But the future buildings destined to replace the vacated and/or dismantled ones are scattered over a multitude of private drawing boards, and none of them has, as yet, reached the planning-permission stage; as a matter of fact, no foundations have been laid, as yet, under a planning office entitled and trusted to issue such permissions. Site-clearing powers seem to have grown considerably; the building industry, however, lags far behind – and the distance between its capacities and the grandiosity of the unattended construction work keeps expanding.

It is the all-too-visible impotence and ineptitude of the extant political machinery that is thus far the principal force prompting people – in steadily growing numbers – to go and to stay on the move. That force's capacity for integration is, however, confined to the ground-clearing operation. It does not extend to the designers, architects and builders of the polis to be erected thereafter. Our 'interregnum' is marked by the dismantling and discrediting of the institutions which have till now serviced the processes of forming and integrating public visions, programmes and projects. After being subjected, together with the rest of the social fabric of human cohabitation, to the processes of thorough deregulation, fragmentation and privatization, such institutions remain stripped of a large part of their executive capacity and most of their authority and trustworthiness, with only a slim chance of getting them back.

Any creation is all but unthinkable unless preceded by, or coterminous with, an act of destruction. Destruction, however, does not by itself determine the nature of a constructive sequel or even makes its imminence a foregone conclusion. As far as the institutional network of society is concerned – and in particular the vehicles of collective, integrated undertakings – it feels as if the year 2011 contributed considerably to the volume and capacity of available bulldozers, whereas the production of construction cranes together with the rest of the building equipment plunged in that year even deeper into the already protracted recession, while existing supplies have been kept idle – put into mothballs in expectation of more propitious times – which, alas, seem stubbornly reluctant to appear.

Leaders of ad hoc coalitions can be only ad hoc leaders – not an attractive job for people with genuine leadership quality, equipped with more than just personal photogenic charm and wheeler-dealing skills, and an appetite for instant, if fragile, noto-riety. Each set of external circumstances creates its own set of realistic options for individual choices, but each option appeals to its own category of potential takers. The manifestly impotent politics which is concerned mainly with keeping its subjects at a safe distance, increasingly run by spin doctors and stage-managers of photo opportunities, and ever more remote from grass-roots daily concerns and worries, is hardly a magnet for individuals with visions and projects reaching beyond the next election date – individuals with qualities indispensable for political leaders, as distinct from political machine-operators. Potential political leaders have not stopped being born; it is the deteriorating and increasingly decadent and powerless political structures that prevent them from coming of age.

Allow me to quote from my *This is not a diary*:

> Alliances collated in the phase of ground-clearing (rainbow-like coalitions of otherwise incompatible interests, notoriously inclined to dissipate shortly after the outpour that put them in place comes to a halt) may well fall promptly apart or even explode, uncovering – for everybody to see – the truth of their ad hoc, marriage-of-convenience nature. The ground-clearing phase has no need for strong leaders: quite on the contrary, strong leaders with strong vision and strong convictions may only bring such rainbow-like coalitions to collapse well before the ground-clearing tasks have been completed. Spokesmen for the people on the move may declare being satisfied (though not necessarily for the right reasons) of neither needing nor having leaders – indeed viewing the leader-less condition of people on the move as a sign of political progress and one of their foremost achievements. Vladimir Putin, when declaring (in all likelihood prematurely) the defeat of massive public protest against the haughty contempt with which the Russian powers-that-be treat their electorate, hit the nail on its head when imputing that alleged failure of the opposition to the absence of a leader capable to put together a program which the protesters would be willing to accept and able to support.

I believe that, censuring/deriding the indignant for appointing no leaders, Putin summed up pretty accurately the current phase in which we are experimenting with alternative tools of effective political action in order to replace the outdated ones that are becoming ever less potent and more rickety. But how long his diagnosis may remain valid for, is not for him – nor as a matter of fact for anyone – to determine, before the people who make history, while being made by it, decide – whether by design or by default. While they are doing it, the urgent, imperative need, as well as likelihood, of genuine political and spiritual leaders will become more and more evident. And then the prospective leaders would do well to recall and learn from Václav Havel's experience and accomplishment; because, even among the most outstanding political figures of recent times, Havel, as it were, stood out.

Unlike other bona fide political leaders, Havel had at his disposal none of the equipment deemed indispensable for exercising tangible influence. There was no massive political movement behind him, complete with ramified and well-entrenched political machinery. He had no access to generous public funds. No army, missile launchers or police, whether secret or uniformed, were there to make his word flesh. There was no mass media to render him a celebrity, to convey his messages to millions and make millions eager to listen and to follow. As a matter of fact, Havel had but three weapons to use in his effort to change history: hope, courage and stubbornness – weapons which all of us possess in one measure or another. The sole difference between Václav Havel and the rest of us is that we, unlike Havel, seldom reach for those weapons; and when (if) we do, we do it with much less – weaker and shorter-lived – determination.

Let me note once more that, however much they were at loggerheads with each other, all great ideologies of the past political spectrum agreed on one point: while ferociously quarrelling about what was to be done, they hardly ever squabbled over the issue of who was going to do whatever in their opinion needed to be done. And there was no need to quarrel, as it was deemed self-evident that the agency bound to make the word flesh was the state: the all-powerful state, as people then believed – a state blending power to do things with the ability to decide which things were to be done and which were to be avoided, and exercising full sovereignty – that is, executive capacity – over its territory and the population that inhabited it. The simple recipe for getting things done (whatever those things might be) was to take over the state apparatus in order to deploy the power it held. Power was visualized as 'stored' in governmental warehouses and ready to use (symbolized in the public imagination by the key for releasing nuclear missiles which any of the successive US presidents has the right to press regardless of the political party that put him into the Oval Office). Whoever administers that warehouse has the capacity to do whatever he/she considers to be right and proper or just expedient.

This is no longer the case, though. Power to get things done floats in the 'space of flows' (Manuel Castells); it is evasive, highly mobile, infuriatingly difficult to locate, pinpoint or fix, and, like the legendary hydra, has many heads. It is immune to locally set and territorially confined rules – and formidably resistant to all attempts to control its movement and render its moves, or its responses to one's own moves, predictable. The flip side is the rapidly declining authority of state governments, displaying daily – yet each day more spectacularly – their impotence. I guess that the fact that visions of 'good society' have fallen out of fashion is ultimately a consequence of the powers able to put such visions in place falling out of sight. Why bother racking one's brain trying to answer the question 'What to do?' if there is no answer to the question 'Who'll do it?'?! We are currently going through multiple crises, but the most acute of them – indeed a 'meta-crisis' which makes all the rest of the crises all but insoluble – is the *crisis of agency* – or, more to the point, of the 'agency as we know it' – the bequeathed and extant agency of the state, tried and tested by past generations who put it together and expected us, as recommended successors, to use it.

Corresponding and complementary to the decline and lapse of (effective, trustworthy) agency was a seminal shift in the realm of ideology. Until a half-century or so ago, ideologies were, so to speak, 'wrapped around' the state – its concerns and set purposes. Today's ideologies are wrapped around the *absence* of the state as an effective instrument of action and change. In its extreme form, present-day ideology is 'privatized' – focused on cutting out a relatively solid/tranquil niche amidst quicksand, a safe and secure shelter inside a hopelessly and incurably unsafe and insecure social setting (like building a family nuclear shelter in a world bent on MAD – 'Mutually Assured Destruction' – or buying oneself into 'gated communities' inside rife-with-violence and unstoppably

decaying cities). At some distance from the pole of extreme 'individualization' and pulverization of social totalities extends a wide
range of ideologies preoccupied with searching for / testing new
forms of collective action as possible alternative(s) to the state
which is conspicuous mostly by its absence. The phenomenon of
'people on the move' is one of these ideologies-in-action. Inchoate
and precocious, obviously not fully formed, more a groping in the
dark than a determined and consistent move in a direction previously designed/chosen, it is thus far at the testing stage. The evidence gathered during the test is, to say the least, ambiguous, and
the jury is still out; in all probability, it will stay out for a considerable time to come. Signals are controversial, the fate of successive tests changes kaleidoscopically, and the contents of their
messages are chameleon-like. The refusal to invest hopes in the
extant political institutions is perhaps their sole invariable and
integrating factor.

The end of history?

Carlo Bordoni　The end of the grand narratives that Lyotard
mentioned has to do with the end of history – according to Fukuyama's apocalyptic vision – thus recuperating the black thread that
connects Nietzsche to postmodernity.[21] The grand narratives are
nothing but the cultural sedimentation in the collective imagination of events which in the past marked significant turning points
or to which was attributed, in retrospect, a special meaning in
order to build the uniformity of the overall picture. Feeling that
he was part of history often legitimized man's choices, by making
him feel that they were right and necessary – though inevitably
led by progress which, like a tireless machine, grinds everything
and carries on in any case, regardless of the human will. As
recalled by Gianni Vattimo, quoting Benjamin, history is always
written by the victors which leaves it open to be manipulated and
ordered from the point of view of the observer.[22]

It follows that the same idea of progress (a modernist idea) is
something forced, an artifice, purpose-built to give legitimacy to
those in power – whether it is an established power or a power in
the making: the great invention of Marxism, which demonstrates
the extraordinary intellectual gifts of its founder, was to give the

proletariat a historical function, linked to the idea of inevitable progress, which made it, even psychologically, the winner-elect of a struggle for social dominance. This was an inevitable process because it was part of human progress, despite 'unhistorical' difficulties and the resistance of the reactionary bourgeoisie. History as a documentary legitimization of the winners, with their unique and universal vision of the history of the planet: a perverse effect caused by an increase in the speed of communications, in what McLuhan called the *global village*, where everyone knows everyone, and where it is no longer acceptable to have different *histories* that change *ad usum* of the various winners. That progress which modernity intended as a guarantor of development in all senses turned out, through real-time communication, to be the most formidable opponent in history, showing the bias of the visions and the inconsistency of the various 'centrisms'.

History has made the news and so it is more and more immediate, objective, but also short-lived. It is easy to forget and replace with the next piece of news, in a rapid process that loses sight of the whole and therefore offers an image that is still topical, vivid, but fragmented, incoherent and contradictory. The question remains whether this vision of reality is better – transitory but real – or if it is better to have the version of history written by the victors, which imposes a structured and reassuring overview – because memory is a source of security. Since the time of Herodotus, history has represented the collective memory as the basis on which to build the identity of a people, assert its true culture and establish its traditions, laws, customs and behaviour. In the modern era, history, blessed by Hegelianism, has consolidated the states, each with its own legitimizing national history, justifying its progress and the need for a form of industrialization geared towards economic growth. The breaking down of trust in a history that postmodernism denounced – in a strikingly different biased form – has contributed to the climate of uncertainty, eliminating that sense of community on the march towards the progress that modernity had pointed to. This is also why the individual has found himself even more alone when suddenly faced with an unknowable and adverse world, because he is deprived of a sense of history and self-awareness.

From Nietzsche to Heidegger, the forerunners of postmodernity, history was regarded more as an imposture than a memory of the truth, and substituted by the event. The event is what happens because of man's actions, but the set of events does not make history because they are detached from each other; they are not bound by a conscious purpose, but are due to the will and personal choices of that time, dictated by opportunity, by needs, by intuition or by pure intention.

The event has no memory: it has value in itself and for the period in which it takes place. It is not repeatable and its truth lies in the impossibility of repeating itself. It is unique and therefore universal. This approach, besides emptying history of its meaning, implicitly denies any value to the evocation of the past, seen as a warning not to repeat mistakes. If every event is unique in its own right, it makes no sense to use it as a means to deter others from repeating facts of the same kind.

And indeed the memory of mistakes (and of horror) does not prevent other mistakes, in different conditions, at different times, for different reasons. If history could really serve to prevent the recurrence of unpleasant events, thanks to the power of memory, we would not have had, for some time now, wars or mass killings, or even racism, marginalization or oppression.

After the destructive phase culminating in postmodernity, now the new history or what replaces it, as a collective memory, is a digital trail that runs through the entire planet and records every human expression, regardless of the social importance of the issuer. Everything becomes part of this universalized and unanimous history (which cannot be contained in one or more books because it is continuously being enriched and is perpetually evolving), demonstrating that history cannot be written by the victors. Its boundless expansion and its fragility make it tenuous to the point of no longer being interpretable. Perhaps for the first time it will be the history of the vanquished, but it is pointless trying to legitimize them.

The electronic trails that we leave behind are the traces of our passage in the world, an alternative way of making history that has taken the place of manuals prepared by specialists, but they are not the only clues. Other, equally significant, signs are recorded and stored by cameras placed all over the city, along the highways, in artificial satellites and, finally, in drones, those miniature environmental recorders in the shape of harmless insects. They collect billions of pieces of information and fill up a huge database, which would require a disproportionate number of analysts to check through it.

A huge memory amounts to a useless memory, because it can only be consulted in part, running the risk of getting a partial and distorted view of reality. However, it has the advantage of keeping the population in a state of constant alert: knowing that there is perpetual monitoring, no one can feel safe; no one is protected from prying eyes even within their own four walls. It creates a sort of universal *Panopticon*, where everyone knows they are being observed, even without seeing the observer, who remains hidden from view, discreet, quiet, in the background, and yet more devious and tenacious than the guard in Jeremy Bentham's prison.

Its thousands of electronic eyes can not only scrutinize every moment of our lives, but also find out about moments of our more or less distant past: like our guilty conscience, always making us feel guilty for what we have done or not done, what we may have forgotten or may have omitted, mistaken or confused. The meaning of the new history, instead of being a general overview of an entire community as a whole, is transformed into a chaotic sum of personal actions, divided, fragmented and useless for future understanding: a set of events, the sense of which, in the long run, disperses and amounts to confusion. For this reason, the most recent event, the topical, the new, represents the face of truth and defeats the prior event. All that has been, though it is recorded in the mass memory, indelible and fixed forever on electronic media, tastes obsolete and is therefore rejected by the social conscience that lives an eternal present, which is continuously renewed.

Memory is therefore no longer an integral part of consciousness, the fundamental nucleus to which we refer in order to decide, to think, to act, to choose, to plan, but something discarded and relegated outside of oneself to an adequate technological support. The experts will resort to it for their research or will browse through it like an old photo album, whose images appear a little blurred, with unrecognizable features.

Tomorrow's society is a society without memory, destined to repeat the mistakes of the past and exhaustingly rebuild its own experience from scratch, but so different from the modern society that we left behind that even the mistakes of the past, thus repeated, will appear in a new light, as if never seen before. So profound is the change that occurred with the end of modernity and so rapid are the innovations that past experience can serve little purpose. It is simply archaeology and, as such, should be preserved in museums.

Postmodernity has been characterized by the crisis of the foundations on which modernity was supported: ideology, history and the work ethic disappoint, resulting in an irreparable rift with the past and causing different, often conflicting, reactions, designed to regain at least social control, given that it is not possible immediately to provide new values and a new ethic. Postmodernity, therefore, is a moment of generalized disorientation, in which there is a chaotic rush for cover in the face of a social context that is no longer defined, stable, reliable and certain.

This is why we cannot call ourselves *modern*, nor even *postmodern*, which implies a relationship of dependency on and opposition to modernity, but are inhabitants of a world that is changing, who call this change 'crisis'.

Zygmunt Bauman   If there is something fully and truly immortal in human history, it is the idea of an imminent end. At almost any time in history someone, somewhere, expected an impending end to something – perhaps at no time more than as in the years preceding the end of the first millennium, the date of Apocalypse. In the modern era, what was expected to end (or, more exactly, to be put an end to) is history – understood as a series of contingencies, an unanticipated product of blind forces. Alongside the already mentioned determination to take the world under a new – this time human – management went the hope/expectation of disposing of the mess and disarray for which history was notorious, starting from scratch, thanks to the rationality of 'new men' who subjected the future flow of time to a designed, closely monitored and therefore transparent pattern. Fukuyama was but the latest in the long line of soothsayers predicting the same. Beside announcing the end of history, he is known as well for pronouncing the impending, long-awaited, arrival of the new man, finally cleansed of the shortcomings that plagued the men and women of old. There was nothing wrong, Fukuyama insisted, with the twentieth-century, essentially sound, intention to create a 'new and improved' human race – the sole snag was that the tools adequate to the task were not yet available. Education, propaganda, brain-washing were all primitive, cottage-industry instruments, no match for the grandiosity of the challenge. The new technology of genetic engineering, fast becoming available, will do the job the old tools were not up to. And once more, as if we learned nothing from the gruesome past, there is no room for a warning that treating humanity as a garden crying out for more beauty and harmony inevitably divides humans into Chelsea-Show specimens and weeds.

Things linger, even if we do not remember them – let alone recall them, chew them over, debate them. They live in what we do and how we do it. Modernity lives, and so does postmodernity, as its shadowy parent/offspring, inner demon and guide. When you finish by defining us as 'inhabitants of a world that is changing, who call this change "crisis"', you are saying as much – or as little – as a responsible person has the right and the duty to say.

You may know that, after weighing the benefits he brought and the harms he has done to his fellow humans, I am not particularly fond of Nietzsche's heirloom as a whole. But among the few of his pronouncements which I cherish – one of the best ever made on the subject – is a terse and concise 'career report' on the human condition, written in 1883 (in *Thus Spake Zarathustra*), yet remarkably correct in 2013.

> Man is a rope, fastened between animal and Superman – rope over an abyss.
> A dangerous going-across, a dangerous wayfaring, a dangerous looking-back, a dangerous shuddering and staying-still.

The stuff of which Nietzsche's rope is braided is what in its raw state we call 'history'. But it is the act of being entwined that recycles the yarn into a rope that can be fastened (this is precisely what the 'collective memory' is currently doing, when processed by politics), though the selection of poles to which it should be fastened depends on the rope-makers rather than the yarn they use, as has been the case for some time now, and as it will continue to be. With due effort, one can fasten the rope to a wide variety of poles, thereby making of historical memory an ally in converting people to one's cause – while using the self-fulfilling and self-defeating capacities of prophecies to co-opt people's action into the service of that cause. Robert Merton, credited with coining the idea while following W. I. Thomas' insight that 'If men define situations as real, they are real in their consequences',[23] defined self-fulfilling prophecy as 'in the beginning a *false* definition of the situation evoking a new behaviour which makes the original false conception come "true". This specious validity of the self-fulfilling prophecy perpetuates a reign of error. For the prophet will cite the actual course of events as proof that he was right from the very beginning.'[24]

There is no wonder that the current main use of the rope(s) visualized by Nietzsche is in the tug-of-war known by the name of power struggle.

Notes

1 J.-F. Lyotard, *The Postmodern Condition: A Report on Knowledge*, trans. G. Bennington and B. Massumi, Manchester University Press, 1984, p. 3.

2 J.-J. Rousseau to Voltaire, 18 August 1756, from J. A. Leigh (ed.), *Correspondance complète de Jean Jacques Rousseau*, vol. IV, trans. R. Spang, Geneva, 1967, pp. 37–50.

3 S. Hessel, *Time for Outrage!* (2010), Quartet Books, 2011.

4 J. Gray, *The Silence of Animals: On Progress and Other Modern Myths*, Allen Lane, 2013, pp. 57–62.

5 É. de la Boétie, *The Politics of Obedience: The Discourse of Voluntary Servitude*, trans. H. Kurz, Skyler J. Collins, 2005.

6 Lyotard, *The Postmodern Condition*.

7 A.-L.-C. Destutt de Tracy, "Elements of Ideology", in *A Treatise on Political Economy*, ed. T. Jefferson, Ulan Press, 2012.

8 See J. Gray, *The Silence of Animals*, p. 98.

9 S. Freud, *The Future of an Illusion*, trans. J. A. Underwood and S. Whiteside, Penguin, 2004, pp. 38–9.

10 C. Jencks, *The Language of Post-Modern Architecture*, Rizzoli, 1977.

11 R. Venturi, D. Scott Brown and S. Izenour, *Learning from Las Vegas*, MIT Press, 1972.

12 Z. Bauman and K. Tester, *Conversation with Zygmunt Bauman*, Polity, 2001, p. 71.

13 R. Sennett, *The Corrosion of Character: The Personal Consequences of Work in the New Capitalism*, W. W. Norton & Co., 1998, p. 51.

14 Ibid., p. 47.

15 Z. Bauman, *Collateral Damage: Social Inequalities in a Global Age*, Polity, 2011.

16 Sennett, *Corrosion of Character*, p. 24.

17 G. Vattimo, *The End of Modernity: Nihilism and Hermeneutics in Postmodern Culture* (1985), Polity, 1992.

18 Cf. A. W. Gouldner, *The Coming Crisis of Western Sociology*, Basic Books, 1970.

19 J. Habermas, *The Philosophical Discourse of Modernity. Twelve Lessons* (1985), trans. F. Lawrence, Polity, 1990.

20 Z. Bauman, *Liquid Modernity*, Polity, 2000.

21 F. Fukuyama, *The End of History and the Last Man* (1992), Penguin, 2012.

22 Vattimo, *End of Modernity*, pp. 8–9.

23 W. I. Thomas, *The Child in America: Behavior Problems and Programs*, Alfred A. Knopf, 1928, p. 572.

24 R. K. Merton, *Social Theory and Social Structure*, Free Press, 1968, p. 477.

3

Democracy in Crisis

We now have a global overclass which makes all the major eco-
nomic decisions, and makes them in entire independence of the
legislatures, and a fortiori of the will of the voters, of any given
country.

Richard Rorty[1]

Ethics of progress and democracy

Carlo Bordoni   That the structure of society was based on economic relations was proven by Marx with the theory of historical
materialism, and for a time was a common belief which it was
pointless even debating. In more recent years, coinciding with the
crisis of modernity, the attractive and liberating hypothesis has
been put forward that the economy is not structural, but depends
on 'available' human factors like culture and other forms of
immaterial production, with which it enters into a dialectical
relationship.

   The economy, in short, no longer represents the real soul of
society, but is one of its many components, and modifiable
like the others. First to support this idea were the revolutionary
thinkers of the Frankfurt School,[2] to whom we owe the seed of
a momentous change – namely, the view that culture, so far

considered to be superstructural (and therefore dependent on the economy), could instead influence and even determine the choices of economic policy: such a strong culture that it could become by itself a structure in a society free from capitalist domination.

What sociologists of the Frankfurt School envisaged after World War II, in the wake of a renewed Enlightenment that succeeded the Nazi–Fascist obscurantism, had to be confirmed by new libertarian and progressive innovations which resulted in the 'cultural revolution' of 1968, when Sartre's insight played a crucial role on the path of the power of imagination, opened by Adorno and Horkheimer.[3] The completed revelation of the human capacity to think, to dream and to imagine its own destiny and break the mould of the past.

The strongly utopian component of this assumption seemed to be confirmed by the trends observed in the society of the 1970s and 1980s, in which a combination of several factors, including the development of technology, post-Fordism and the dematerialization of work, as well as the explosion of consumerism and spread of communications, opened society to a collective participation.

During the years of the successive stages of transition, in addition to great uncertainty, confusion and inevitable misunderstandings, we also had the sensation that here was an extraordinary opportunity for choice. The immense, exciting opportunity to decide one's own future is generally bound to cause acute disappointment once we became aware that the path taken is not the desired one, that the decisions were taken elsewhere – that, once again, destiny, that is, the historical situation, proper to the time in which man is living, is independent of our choices.

What happened after that euphoric phase, which coincided in part with the end of modernity, is there for all to see. Postmodernism has given us the illusion of living in a world free from needs, free from ideologies, open to the promises of unlimited consumerism, of a dazzling spectacle, of exaltation of individuality in exchange for job insecurity, uncertainty, loneliness.

The economy has regained control of society, and has fully resumed its dominant, structural role. What looked like a certain decline was only a temporary blackout, a strategic retreat while it waited to come back to the forefront.

Of course, the economy has also changed; it has had to adapt to the times and support the weight of the crisis of modernity. The players have changed but, as they say, the song remains the same. Not only is it a postindustrial economy, which lost along the way the unique characteristics of a system based on factories, large plants, concentrations, long-term investments and keeping the work force faithful, but it is also a postcapitalist one, in the sense that capitalism has lost its close ties with the world of work.

It is also dematerialized; it has, so to speak, released itself from large investments, from large industrial projects to which it was committed long-term, and it has turned to the financial markets, which are in a virtual place, therefore a *non-place*, which does not have a geographical location, but moves freely at higher levels, above territories and earthly things, with a frenetic, immediate mobility, responsive to every changing signal.

If the *proletariat* has become the *precariat*, marked by the uncertainty of employment, in a similar way the capitalist is no longer the *master* – that is, he who owns the means of production. Ownership of the machines, which is inseparable from the process of industrialization, was what once made the difference between the master and the worker. Now the investment of large sums of capital in the purchase of expensive machinery for industry is no longer advantageous, in that it does not correspond to a *stable* and *secure* status: even for the entrepreneur, the margins of uncertainty have expanded and become almost uncontrollable. Long-term successful investment in manufacturing depends no longer on courage, inventiveness and financial liquidity, but on external factors, including, on the one hand, the rapid obsolescence of the technology used, and, on the other, the instability of the markets, the stock market, the banks, and even the laws of the state itself, which – instead of ensuring, as in the past, a climate of stability and providing a clearing house in times of economic difficulties, to restore balance, subsidize with public money and mediate to maintain employment levels – is concerned about its own stability.

The state is going through a profound crisis of identity: far from recuperating its relationship of trust with the public, who had been informed of its constitution right from the beginning, it has to bear the repercussions of the crisis of modernity, which drags it into undeserved degradation, accompanied – as in every phase of decline – by corruption, and mistrust on the part of the people. The current political crisis (defined as *anti-political*) is the crisis of the modern state. Worried about how to defend the reasons for its existence, it moves to regain credibility by reducing public debt and implementing a neoliberal policy, forgetting that its primary purpose is not to balance the budget, but to provide adequate services to the citizen.

Given that the neoliberal choice adopted, which is highly unfeasible for a public body, may give the expected results of severity and confidence, it is not able to ensure the kind of intervention in the economy which, at other times, had allowed for large industries to be met halfway in order to avoid unemployment.

The alliance between state and private industry has for a long time been one of the most solid pillars of modernity, ensuring an effective balance between political expediency, economic needs, employment and social control. This was seen right from the time when large industrial family-owned enterprises emerged in the nineteenth century, and reconfirmed by the policies of the post-war totalitarian governments and democracies, proving to be a sacred alliance that has provided stability to the entire Western society, until the presuppositions of that close tie broke down as a consequence of globalization that has led, as regards the state, to the separation of power and politics, and, as regards industry, to the dematerialization of work.

Capital has been freed from work, from investments which turned out to be less and less profitable, both because of the greater uncertainty of the markets (the restriction in consumption is creating serious problems for economic equilibrium), and the increase in labour costs – not to mention the banking restrictions, which reduce short-term credit, bringing about a lack of liquidity for operating needs. Added to this is the already mentioned breaking of the alliance with the state and the constant threat of legislative changes, the need to adapt to new safety regulations, fiscal crackdowns and VAT rates. This is an obstacle course to which weaker businesses have responded by closing down; those in a stronger position have reacted by reducing the work force or by moving to a different geographical location, transferring their plants and management to developing countries where labour is cheap. There, controls are slacker and, indeed, local governments have a certain economic margin to encourage the setting up of new businesses. A temporary solution, perhaps, which will last until the effects of globalization are felt there too, triggering the same problems encountered in the country of origin.

The liquidation of capital invested in industry and its transfer to the empyrean of supranational finance is a recent phenomenon, but one that is already well established and of proven reliability. Compared to the fixed assets of the past, to their visible materiality, translated into machinery, plants, factories, pollution and labour, financial capital is intangible, volatile and without an owner. In fact, it does not correspond to specific individuals who have a name and a face; we must not imagine it as subjected to the inflexible inspection of an old gentleman with a top hat, sitting at his desk on the top floor of the headquarters of a holding company. There are no owners – only company executives who move virtual money extremely quickly: invest and disinvest, buy and sell according to market principles, within an unfathomable web of exchanges, relations, transactions, which still produce profit. They register higher profits than any investment industry, and with less responsibility. The consequences of financial transactions and market decisions are equally significant; they make an equally profound impact on people's lives, are decisive in making or breaking people's fortunes – usually making it increasingly difficult to survive – but no one is held accountable.

The takers of financial decisions are immune from objective liability, above all moral ethics, which are not the ethics of profit. Only to the latter are they accountable. Just as the ancient kings and despots did not care about the lives of their subjects whom they sent to die in battle to satisfy their whims, so the anonymous men of virtual finance have no liability for the damages caused by their actions.

If the stock market falls and burns billions, wiping out in one fell swoop the investors' savings, no one really cares. There is always someone who makes money out of every loss. Financial capital flies too far above our heads to be seen and kept under control. It is distanced from the defensive measures of national states, moving quickly from one part of the globe to another, determining the fate of millions of people.

Together with ideology, the work ethic was one of the foundations of modernity. Used to construct the identity of modern man, it emerged as a result of the consolidation of the industrial revolution and has endured for centuries to come. The idea of *progress* is a modern idea: it means that every human action is aimed at improvement, and that history itself is the bearer of a thrust in this direction.

While seemingly inherent in human nature, especially since the dawn of the individual's self-awareness, the idea of progress is in fact a relatively recent concept. For the Greeks and Latins, the issue simply did not arise. They saw in the future signs of a change that should be avoided and turned to the past, to a mythical golden age from which man had fallen. Plato saw this as a period of decline, according to a theory of the degeneration of widely shared politics, the result of conservatism that dreams of a return to the simplicity of natural existence. Others, like Aristotle, theorized a doctrine of historical cycles that are repeated countless times. Horace could write 'Damnosa quid non imminuit dies' (What is there that corroding time does not damage?), in the belief that time is the enemy of man, who can only expect the worst from the future.

This constant looking to the past, typical of the classics, is attributed to the impossibility of going beyond the restricted limits of human experience. Locked in their horizon they could not see beyond or go beyond that experience and imagine the future. Despite the exceptions of Democritus and Epicurus, who did not believe in the golden age, a general sense of pessimism prevailed, and even in Lucretius, where the concept of 'progress' ('pedetemptim progredientis') appears for the first time in *De rerum natura*,[4] the apocalyptic prospect of a world destined to come to an end is accepted.

To find a change of direction, we must look to the dawn of the seventeenth century and Bacon, whose introduction of the inductive method in science reveals the first symptoms of modernity, in which the end of knowledge is utility ('commodis humanis inservire': 'mitigating man's suffering for the advancement of his happiness'), taken up by Fontenelle, Cartesio, Hobbes and Spinoza, and later to flourish in the Age of Enlightenment with Montesquieu, Voltaire and Turgot.

Resulting from a single Enlightenment matrix, the idea of progress has taken different routes following irreconcilable ideologies. The modernist, and more markedly liberal, idea, on the path indicated by Adam Smith, is bound to the principles of free trade, leading to consumerism, while, following the path from Hegel to Marx, which is bound to the concept of history, progress aims at liberation from want and from state control. Both visions were destined to enter into crisis in the second half of the following century: one in relation to the commodification of values; the other following the collapse of the communist regimes.

The simultaneity of both these events suggests that there is a common root, which can be connected with the crisis of modernity and, therefore, of the fundamental principles upon which the essence of modernity is based: faith in technology, hope for a continuous improvement of human existence, belief in ideologies. Put simply, trust in progress.

In a text from the 1920s, the Irish historian John B. Bury showed that the idea of progress is linked to the dominant ideologies of the moment and pursues the utopian project of an ideal society, whose characteristics change substantially over time.[5]

There can be no opposition to the inevitable historical process – writes Marx, who was one of the most acute interpreters of modernity – and it is good that humanity marches solidly towards *the red sunrise of the future*: that is, towards a future which, albeit gradually and slowly, leads to the realization of human happiness – liberation from fatigue and necessity, with the guarantee of equality between men and the elimination of private property. This happiness – both in the Marxist context and the bourgeois one (the daughter of Protestantism) – was promised as feasible on the land itself. It would be a tangible result of conquest, of struggle and hard work: a much closer and more achievable objective than the aleatory, spiritual one, which – in the centuries before the industrial revolution – the Church had promised after death. The work ethic, the bourgeois ethic, is far more pragmatic in offering, here and now, a reward for a life well spent in the *sanctity* of work.

Moreover, the work ethic offered man a personal identity to be proud of, which could ensure dignity even to the humblest worker, who could identify himself with his job. Marx's proletariat – united in class-consciousness (a historically innovative term) – by virtue of the dignity of the work they do, could aspire to liberation from need and expect to subvert the order of industrialized society, taking over its power. If such a society is founded on work (as we read in many constitutions), it is logical that the workers would expect to be leading it.

The work ethic has been the most effective invention of modernity because it has managed to achieve a dual purpose without the need for continuity with the religious spirit of the past, with which it reached an implicit agreement, integrating with it to become its secular arm.

In the first place, by assigning a moral value, as well as an economic one, to manual labour and the consequent personal sacrifice, it ensured a limitless and replaceable mass labour force for the growing industrialization. Second, by eliminating much of the vagrancy and unemployment, it reduced the risk of sedition, riots and crimes against property, thus helping to ease the social burden of the maintenance of the marginalized, the poor, the sick and the criminal.

In the non-industrialized economy (agricultural or pastoral) work was seen as a vital necessity: people worked as much as was necessary to have enough to eat and so to survive. With industrialization, with work becoming a form of identity and a moral obligation, people work more than necessary, causing that particular distortion discussed by André Gorz, whereby hard labour is borne in exchange for *sublimated satisfaction*: money, which can buy pleasure that waged labour is not able to provide.[6]

What was a mirage for workers in the eighteenth and nineteenth centuries began to appear more clearly at the beginning of the twentieth: department stores turned on the electric lights and displayed their shop windows on the streets, creating heaven on earth. All that everyone could wish for was finally at hand, available on the shelves at affordable prices. For those who did not have enough money, the possibility of bank credit was offered to them. The advantages were immediate, while repayment could be made in convenient instalments.

That was the apotheosis of modernity: consumerism for everyone – with no exceptions. Wasn't this happiness, after all? Wasn't this all that you could desire from life – to have, to buy and to consume what you want, without limits and without guilt? The work ethic had come to reward the virtuous consumer, who spends everything he earns to strengthen the productive economy and the markets. In this way, consumerism got ready to take on greater importance with respect to production and to become, in late modernity, the great alternative to work itself.

It took two centuries to achieve this result and they were centuries of struggle, sacrifice and hardship in order to deserve the happiness of consuming in peace. The logic of the string 'more work, more income, more consumption, equals greater satisfaction for all' (not only for the workers) has supported many trade union disputes within the ethics imposed by modernity, whose requests were directed more towards wage increases, rather than an improvement in the quality of life. Their aim was achieving greater economic equality between employer and employee, implicitly accepting the rules of a game based on the quantity and not on the quality of the work. Therefore, the work ethic is responsible for the most large-scale economic phenomenon that occurred in the last century: consumerism. More money, more purchasing power, led to more material wealth. Let's not mention that the quantitative logic is quickly recuperated by the system: a general increase in salary always corresponds to a consequent increase in consumer prices. The balance cannot be altered that much. After all, at least this promise was kept. However, the paradise of consumerism has turned out to be ephemeral.

This can be blamed on the mechanism of growth, a manifestation of endless progress, which results in the acquisition of new goods, services and perishable items, whose possession and use give the feeling of completion and satisfaction with life – though all at the expense of the resources of the planet in which we live and which – in contrast to the idea of progress instilled three centuries ago, when the problem did not arise – are not endlessly available; for the most part they are not renewable. The acknowledgement of the limits to mindless consumption – the hyperconsumerism analysed by Gilles Lipovetsky[7] – has led to a rethinking of the idea of continuous growth and of the *idea of progress* itself, contributing to the consideration that the period of modernity, which was based on these concepts, has come to an end. The new idea of progress was no longer based on the amount of wealth produced, nor on the increase in sales and consumption but, according to Serge Latouche, on the quality of life.[8]

Edgar Morin even talks of a 'domination of progress', which is replaced by a culture of the immediate.[9] In this sense, progress is an *escape from the past*, full of hope that what will happen tomorrow will, in any case, go beyond the present. A culture of the immediate is the natural consequence of the collapse of certainties about the problematic issues of our time. We no longer believe that the future can guarantee an improvement in how we live; we look to the future with worry and suspicion. We cling to the present with the anguish of those who are afraid of losing what they have: almost the same attitude as that of the ancient Greeks and Romans, who feared that the future would be worse than the present day.

Zygmunt Bauman   The birth of the idea of 'Progress', of a linear, essentially straight-line and predetermined, unstoppable itinerary of the human condition, from savagery through barbarity to civilization, from serfdom to freedom, from ignorance to knowledge, from submission to nature to the power over nature, and all in all from bad to good, from good to better, from distressing to comfortable and – to put all these hopes/convictions/expectations in a nutshell – from imperfect to perfect, was the hub of the optimistic, self-assured, boisterous and adventurous *Weltanschauung* of the up-and-coming middle class, that third estate that, in Sieyès' memorable declaration, was nothing, but became all.

'Progress' was the faith of Europe at the peak of its power, the Europe of imperialism, world conquest and colonialism, the metropolis of empires on which the sun never set. The idea of progress reached the peak of its domination of the European mind just before the sun started to lower over the horizon ahead of the long – thirty-year-long – dark age which the war between Europeans vying for the redistribution of their overseas assets was about to visit upon the globe, turning it into the battlefield for their domestic enmities.

As I mentioned before, John Gray in *The Silence of Animals* classifies 'progress' as a myth. He writes:

> For those who live inside a myth, it seems a self-evident fact. Human progress is a fact of this kind. If you accept it you have a place in the grand march of humanity. Humankind is, of course, not marching anywhere. 'Humanity' is a fiction composed from billions of individuals for each of whom life is singular and final. But the myth of progress is extremely potent. When it loses its power those who have lived by it – as Conrad put it [in the same

story you quote] 'like those lifelong prisoners who, liberated after many years, do not know what use to make of their freedoms'. When faith in the future is taken from them, so is the image they have of themselves.[10]

Wandering amidst the ruins of imperialism, colonialism and European hubris, we the Europeans find ourselves – collectively, if not always singly or separately – in the position of Kayerts and Carlier, Conrad's heroes 'who were serving [in the Congo] the cause of progress for up to two years': abruptly liberated – and in the hard way – from the myth's prison – though we took (or were hurled on) another route to where we are now. The outcome is nevertheless much the same, whichever route was taken. We do not know what use to make of our uninvited freedom; we don't even know what freedom is (one knows well what one means by freedom when it is something one still has to fight for) and are not sure whether it is worth defending (one is sure that it is worth defending until the moment it has been won). This leads to confusion, loss of direction; life sliced in self-contained episodes drifting and straying away from each other in an unpredictable manner. All such sentiments, impressions and experiences combine into an 'uncertainty syndrome', twinned with 'incomprehension syndrome'. Staying inside the myth of progress, our ancestors looked towards the future in hope; we look in fear. If a term 'progress' crops up in our thought and talk, it is usually in the context of a threat of being kicked out or falling out of a fast-accelerating vehicle with no fixed timetable, reliable schedule and trustworthy destination sticker. From being a promise of bliss, 'progress' turned into the name of a menace – and of a kind known for its nasty habit of striking without warning and from an unpredictable place. It can be argued that the collapse of trust in the predetermined, and thus assured, 'advancement in the definite and desirable direction', which Bury pinpointed as the very essence of our short yet stormy romance with 'progress', underlies all the rest of the crises affecting the heritage bequeathed by the generations that lived 'inside' that myth to us, doomed to live outside it.

Among that 'rest of the crises', the one affecting the inherited institutions of democracy is arguably the most serious, as it strikes at the sole instruments of collective purposeful action currently at our disposal. We've already discussed that issue under the heading

of the 'crisis of agency': representative democracy within the
framework of a territorial sovereign political unit is paramount
among the agencies we are used to resorting to whenever a collective, purposeful action is needed – that is, daily. For reasons we
have also already discussed, that particular agency can no longer
be trusted to be able, or indeed willing, to deliver on its promise
to follow the will of the electorate that appointed it as its repre-
sentative/plenipotentiary.

Harald Welzer might have been on the right track when in his
discussion of the present-day quandary faced by effective, conse-
quential action aimed at arresting and neutralizing the trends
threatening the future of the planet, our shared home.[11] After
arguing that the problems our planet currently confronts call for
little less than some kind of a cultural revolution – a radical change
in our mode of life – he added that, as 'individualist strategies
have a mainly sedative function [whereas] the level of international politics offers the prospect of change only in a distant
future', 'cultural action is left with the *middle* level, the level of
one's own society, and the democratic issue of how people want
to live in the future'. He suggested as well that popular awareness
that this is the case is on the rise, even if, in many – perhaps most
– cases, it remains rather subliminal or poorly articulated. I believe
that the phenomenon of 'glocalization' – that peculiar combination of localities gaining in importance synchronically (and in
close connection) with spatial distance losing its significance – can
be traced down to the condition correctly diagnosed by Welzer.
And this is why:

The most acute and menacing problems haunting our contemporaries are, as a rule, globally produced by essentially *extraterritorial* forces located in the 'space of flows' (Manuel Castells'
term) which stay well beyond the reach of the essentially local,
territorially fixed political instruments of control; the forces gen-
erating them tend, however, to wash their hands of tackling the
social consequences of their deeds, which are all too often devastating and necessitate urgent and exceedingly costly repairs. This
latter task falls therefore to the 'localities' on the receiving end of
their activities. 'Localities' – and big cities first and foremost
among them – serve nowadays as dumping grounds for problems
generated globally, not by their initiative and without their consultation, let alone agreement.

Immigration, for instance, an un-detachable correlate of pro-gressive 'diasporization' of the planet, is a phenomenon caused by the steadily growing production of redundant people in far-away lands – but it is up to the people in the places of the migrants' arrival to provide them with jobs, accommodation, education facilities and medical care, as well as to mitigate the tensions which the influx of strangers is likely to provoke. Pollution of water supplies or the air might also be a summary – global – consequence of the adverse modes of governance practised in distant countries, but it is ultimately the duty of city authorities to clean the air breathed and the water drunk by the city's resi-dents; rapidly rising costs of health services might be the result of the marketing policies of extraterritorial pharmaceutical compa-nies, but it falls to the local urban authorities to ensure an unbro-ken and adequate provision of hospital and community services.

Ultimately, cities all over the world are turned into local labo-ratories in which ways to resolve these, and numerous other, globally generated problems are improvised or purposefully designed and then put to the test and either rejected or incorpo-rated into daily practice. They are also, again due to an externally created and imposed necessity rather than by a deliberate choice on the part of their residents, cast in the role of research establish-ments and schools for civic responsibility and the difficult art of human cohabitation under novel conditions of irreducible cultural diversity and persistent existential uncertainty. This is what has today stripped 'localities' – big cities more drastically than any others – of a considerable part of their past autonomy and their earlier capacity of composing and running their own agenda – but simultaneously invested them with an unprecedented importance through assigning to them a crucial role in the job of sustaining the present-day global order and correcting its malfunctions and blunders, as well as repairing the collateral damages they are bound to perpetrate. 'Glocalization' means local repair centres servicing and recycling the output of the global problem industry.

There is, however, one more tremendously important role which the 'localities' – and again big cities in particular – are called upon to perform under conditions of glocalization. The two overlapping spaces distinguished by Manuel Castells, the 'space of flows' and the 'space of places', differ radically in the character of inter-human relations which they prompt, favour, promote and encourage. In the former space, humans confront each other primarily as members of 'imagined totalities' (like nation-states, churches or supra-national business interests) – entities a priori separate and self-enclosed, that also hold antagonistic and principally irreconcilable interests locked in reciprocal competition and inclined to beget mutual hostility and suspicion. Having analysed that state of affairs on its own, without reference to the altogether different realities characteristic of the 'space of places', Samuel P. Huntington memorably predicted an imminent 'clash of civilizations' (in 2002, in a book with the same title), pregnant with apocalyptic consequences.[12] One of the most salient effects of glocalization is, however, a human condition suspended between two universes, both subject to sharply distinct sets of norms and rules. Unlike in the 'space of flows', inside the 'space of places' humans have the opportunity of confronting each other as people – neighbours, workmates or schoolmates, bus drivers, postmen or postwomen, shopkeepers, craftsmen, waiters, doctors, dentists, nurses, receptionists, teachers, policemen or policewomen, municipal officers, security guards and so on and so on: some of them are confronted as friends, some others as enemies, but *personal* friends or enemies rather than anonymous and interchangeable, stereotyped specimens of an abstract category.

Of course in our densely populated, heavily diasporized, urban-environment population, most encounters among city dwellers are shallow and perfunctory, seldom reaching deeper than a hasty and superficial, categorial ascription in passing; stereotyping and an a priori reserve underpinned with watchfulness and suspicion tend therefore to be fairly common expedients, resorted to for the sake of self-orientation in the complex, volatile and variegated townscape. A sufficient number of individual specimens of diasporas sharing the city space tend, however, to be drawn out of their anonymity and transferred to the realm of personal, face-to-face acquaintances, for the mental walls separating abstract categories to be pierced and for the outcomes of habitual wholesale stereotyping to be gradually, yet steadily, undermined. If that happens, the customary badges of 'foreigners' (such as skin colour or shade, facial features, ways of dressing and behaving in public, pronunciation and intonation of speech, etc.) become less visible and, in the course of time, tend to be left out of focus – specimens of an alien category being subjected instead to the familiar, personality-related criteria of evaluation of the 'friendly vs unfriendly work-mate or schoolmate', 'helpful vs uncooperative neighbour', or simply 'likeable vs nasty person' kind. As such contacts become, as a consequence, more frequent, and encounters become less perfunctory, the criteria of personal evaluation become indistin-guishable from those routinely applied in selecting or deselecting friends. What counts in the end is the attractiveness of a person and the quality of her or his character, degree of reliability, loyalty or trustworthiness. Features originally registered in order to draw borderlines and dig trenches between 'us' and 'them' are, for all practical intents and purposes, rendered irrelevant to the selection of bonds to be tied – if they are even noticed at all.

And so one more condition for peaceful and mutually beneficial human cohabitation, grossly neglected and even recklessly tram-pled on and reduced to a pulp by the forces floating in the 'space of flows', might be (imperceptibly rather than in the full glare of the spotlight, spontaneously more than according to preconceived plans, prompted by the very logic of urban life and all too often only noticed retrospectively, with the benefit of hindsight) pulled together and firmed up, day in, day out, on the city streets and in public buildings and squares. In this respect, too, Welzer's 'middle level', the 'level of one's own society', may be viewed as a labora-tory inside which future modes of human cohabitation, which have been made indispensable by globalization and emerged thanks to the 'glocalization' form it took, are designed and tested; and also viewed as a school in which urban inhabitants learn how to apply these modes in the practice of shared life.

It is as difficult as it is inadvisable to play down the global role which 'localities' – and they alone – might perform in constructing and putting into operation, as a matter of urgency, the cultural precepts that are so badly needed in order to meet the challenges posed by the 'global interdependence' of the human residents of the planet, and to rise to the task of preventing the planet, together with humanity, from destroying itself. After all, one of the main reasons that Huntington's dark premonitions reverberated so widely and strongly in public opinion was the author and his readers overlooking, or willingly yet mistakenly leaving out of the picture, that 'middle level' that thus far holds our glocalized world together, at the same time serving as a workshop in which the ways and means of rendering its future secure, are sought and stand a chance of being found or developed.

An excess of democracy?

Carlo Bordoni   Does a crisis of democracy exist? Josef L. Fischer, in a book written in the 1930s, considers this to be its normal condition.[13] Today we talk as if this concept had travelled along a trajectory, at the peak of which there was an optimal condition of freedom, which then gradually declined. In reality there has never been a golden age in a democracy: the aspirations, the major theoretical systems and the best of intentions have not exactly been put into practice. The very idea of democracy is a fluctuating, vague one, sometimes indefinable in its complexity.

In modern times it has come to assume an abstract content – like other positive terms, such as *freedom* and *happiness* – and to be used as a passkey or password, a screen to cover up the worst kinds of oppression by man on man. Many forms of government define themselves as democratic without actually being so, with cynical mental reservations and an obvious intent to deceive their fellow citizens, who rally support on the basis of false assumptions and even more false promises. This occurs to such an extent that today the term 'democracy' has been so emptied of its original meaning – *government of the people* – that it is looked upon more and more with jaded scepticism, if not with outright suspicion.

Luciano Canfora noted, not without irony, that, in Roman times, the Greek meaning of 'demokratìa' was 'dominion *over* the people', to the point that Dione Cassius, a historian of the Severi period, referred to the dictator Sulla as 'demokràtor'.[14] The ambiguity is not solved even by going back to the Athens of Pericles, where, by unanimous recognition, the term originated. Here, too, we can see the imposing nature, which is therefore to some extent antithetical to *freedom* – of force used by the people – not understood in its totality, but as the majority. In his observation of the good governance of Pericles, Thucydides recognizes its libertarian character, *despite* the fact that the decisions are taken by majority vote. This already undermines the certainty that democracy coincides with the idea of political perfection that we expect. In short, this *weak point* was already present at the very beginning, and could only cause subsequent conflicts, doubts, ambiguities and the ongoing remedial action that has been implemented through the application of democratic principles.

If we recognize a forced quality in the idea of democracy, or even its character as 'dictatorship' of the many over the few, we will have to admit how difficult it is to reconcile it with the idea of freedom – unless we limit the right to freedom to the circle of those privileged people who have the power to take decisions on behalf of everyone. Also, the majority is a relative concept: we must be wary of speaking of democracy when the decision makers are the majority of male voters or citizens in possession of certain titles or the right assets, or those belonging to a privileged caste, rather than land owners. There has been a variety of options, reservations, conditions and subterfuge that would be unbelievable if it were not borne out by the history books.

And even when, after exhausting struggles, sacrifices and bloodshed, it is possible to apply the principle of universal suffrage, there is still no lack of disappointments. The French socialists of the nineteenth century discovered this to their cost during the experience of the Commune and the subsequent *coup d'état* by Louis Bonaparte. The fact that *everyone* can vote does not guarantee, in itself, a popular victory, nor that the form of government that the elections produce is really in the interests of the people. Since then, the left has been dragging with it this historic mistake, forgetting that there are many ways and tricks for channelling consensus and making it go in the direction that is most convenient to those in power. We only have to think of Fascism and all the great totalitarian regimes that based their success on the exaltation of the masses, on the meaning of sacrifice, on spectacle and ritual. They favoured the indistinct group of the many – very nearly all – but sacrificed individual freedom.

It must have immediately become clear that democracy in the full sense of the term – that is, government of *all* the people – was difficult to implement. In order to avoid chaos, various opportune corrective actions were introduced to reduce the numbers of the ungovernable, including the principle of representation – with many misgivings.

Jean-Jacques Rousseau refers to democracy in the true sense of the classical Athenian democracy in the age of Pericles, which even then had serious problems of compatibility with the idea of freedom, and admits that 'if the term is taken in its strict sense, true democracy has never existed and never will. It is against the natural order that the majority should govern and the minority be governed.'[15] He then goes on to define the limits of representative democracy: 'Sovereignty cannot be represented, for the same reason that it cannot be transferred; it consists essentially in the general will, and the will cannot be represented; it is itself or it is something else; there is no other possibility. The people's deputies are not its representatives, therefore, nor can be, but are only its agents; they cannot make definitive decisions. Any law that the people in person has not ratified is void; it is not a law.'[16]

So, according to the words of Rousseau, democracy does not exist and will never exist, if we consider this term in its real meaning, i.e., 'government by the people'. However, today, when we speak of 'democracy', we mean something else. We are aware that that formula is nothing more than a convention, a formal label we give to something with a more abstract and broad meaning, which contains everything we believe is right, optimal and functional for civil existence. Something that encompasses freedom, solidarity, equality, respect for and observance of the rights of others: a complex idea that, as Morin would say, is greater than the sum of its components.

All this forms in our mind the idea of democracy, an ideal of civil society to strive for and that cannot be measured, unlike progress, in quantitative terms. We must therefore distinguish between the original meaning of 'democracy' as a 'government by the people' (prevalence of the majority), and what we understand today: freedom, equality, respect for minorities.

For the transformation in the current sense of the idea of democracy we have to thank Alexis de Tocqueville, who was the first to waive its etymological meaning to make it take on a broader meaning, of a social nature, indicating rather an idea of equality and a propensity towards the generalized extension of one set of rights and obligations:[17] equality of rights before the state and equal treatment before the law. This was a democracy that tends to eliminate the privileges of the elite, to give everyone the same opportunities, and chances of improvement.

And so, it is a democracy that privileges the individual, as in the cultural tradition of the United States, where the principle of the *self-made man* is deeply rooted, together with the liberal spirit in economics.

The example of America, where democracy takes on this new and unprecedented connotation, which was destined to be accepted and shared throughout the West, topples the idea of the oppressive power of the majority and the fears of lack of freedom which were already present in the time of Pericles. On the one hand, we are witnessing the renunciation of the idea of the strong, almost authoritarian and despotic, overwhelming popular power – which in Marxist theory even manifests itself as a revolutionary force – capable of levelling the entire society and, on the other, a softer conception of democracy is established, in an abstract and ideal sense, intended more to ensure equal rights for all citizens rather than for the majority of them. It is on this double meaning of the term that, after Tocqueville, the destinies of the Western states ride, with continual alternation in predominance of one interpretation or the other, depending on the historical moment and political expediency.

The ambiguity of the term 'democracy', in the scope, complexity and sometimes contradictory nature of the meaning that is attributed to it, lends itself – especially during the second half of the nineteenth and the early twentieth century – to conflicting interpretations, with results which are not always satisfactory. In monarchical or oligarchic, despotic and absolutist regimes, the meaning of democracy is reflected in the strong sense, as a replacement of the people's power by that of one or a few. But then it comes up against the difficulty of managing a government of the assembly type. Similarly, Marxism understood democracy as a 'dictatorship of the proletariat', but then delegated the management of political power to a small minority, to a privileged elite.

The strong idea of democracy was used, however, by the totalitarian regimes of the right to get rid of the disruptive influence of a turbulent, uncontrollable and incompetent mass who presumed, in the name of numbers, to take in hand the destiny of the country. To Fascism and Nazism, democracy, thus understood, was the most serious threat that could be faced by any form of civilization, and it was precisely because they wanted to prevent the masses from erasing the social order that they imposed control through authoritarianism and totalitarianism, extreme and illiberal forms of personal control, aimed at uniformity and conformity. A constant and brutal oppression that, as those regimes fully intended, has the power to manage the mass and at the same time reserve total freedom of expression and actions for the best, for the chosen few: the ruling class, who stand out from the people.

Democracy comes in many shapes, but in modern times, since its assertion thanks to the bourgeois class – 'No bourgeoisie, no democracy', writes Barrington Moore Jr – has chosen a representative form:[18] that is, that special parliamentary democracy that is put into effect not directly, but through the election of representatives. Regardless of how good this formula might be, and beyond any consideration of the legitimacy of representation – a subject which Rousseau had already discussed in *The Social Contract,* claiming the incompatibility of democracy and representation – it is clear that the crisis of modernity has brought with it a crisis of representative democracy.

History teaches us that in any political system in decline, the legal principles remain valid and protected by the State, but are undermined from within by growing corruption and, from the outside, by a loss of confidence among the electorate; this degraded form is destined to linger, at least until the system implodes or is reformed on other grounds.

The introduction of representation, in this respect, cannot be considered a betrayal of democratic principles, but a softening of them – mediation achieved over time that takes into account the needs of the majority, but does not forget the opposition, and tries to safeguard the individual and, therefore, personal freedom, which *kratìa* of the *demo* would have crushed forever.

Mediation is necessary to moderate the ambitions of the captains of the people, the aggressiveness of the masses, the inevitable emotions that accompany every political action. Every time the masses have tried to assert themselves to practise the purest form of *democracy,* opposing injustice, corruption or mismanagement, an inevitable leader immediately materialized. Demagogues, leaders, commanders of the crowds, all were ready to ride the protest, to direct it and to draw almost absolute power from it. The charismatic leader who incites the crowd – history always untiringly produces new examples – is worse than the elected representative.

Any relinquishment of representative democracy would really be the end of the world as we know it: more than a return to basics, it would be a leap of faith whose consequences we are not able to predict. It could open up the most diverse scenarios: from a period of political chaos to the seizing of power by strong governments, consisting of ministers appointed from above, unelected and unqualified politically, or perhaps – something that seems more likely – the elimination of democratic representation, reduced more and more to mere appearance, and replaced by an impersonal 'governance' on a global level, with an increasingly lower degree of interference from politics, and a high degree of social control. This would be much like what is already happening through the tracking of mobile phones, the use of the internet, drones and cameras in cities, only much more sophisticated and complex. Will it still be a democracy (a definition that no one wants to give up)? It might be the perfect democracy, because power will not be represented by an elected group, but by a diffused network of officials who carry out their duty for the greater good. It really would be the power of the people because there wouldn't be anyone on the other side. There would be no opposing party, just a power without a face against which it would be impossible to rebel, because it is split into thousands of small entities (and these would indeed be elective), with whom it will be possible to interact because they are situated at a local level and visible but always changeable and unstable in that they are subordinate to higher orders and not responsible for the choice of paths taken.

According to Charles Tilly, speaking of the governors in office, 'de-democratisation' is a prompt reaction to the crisis of the regime when they see 'a clear threat to their power'.[19] Each time provisions restricting personal freedom, exceptional measures or limited political rights are decreed, it results in an effect of de-democratization. Analyses of this effect have been carried out regularly on an international level since 1972 by Freedom House, a non-governmental organization based in Washington.

The problem always lies in the difficult relationship between central power and popular will. The process of democratization is, in its own way, perverse and mystifying. Both adjectives only partly explain the ambiguity of an idea that originated with a derogatory meaning, in opposition to individual freedom. It subsequently came into everyday language to indicate, with an unusual semantic reversal, the maximum freedom that a form of

government can guarantee its citizens. Democracy as a synonym
for participation, respect for the will of the people, recognition of
political rights, and self-determination through free elections with
universal suffrage was used by governments as a label or certificate
of guarantee against any suspicion of authoritarianism, dictatorship or absolutism.

Sought after, dreamed of, strongly desired, in all times, often
calling for individual sacrifice, democracy has assumed, with
modernity, a wavering ideological sense, depending on the historical, political and social environments in which it has been invoked.

If it is true, as pointed out by Canfora,[20] that, at the end of
World War II, the term 'democracy' was appropriated by all
parties, governments and states that emerged from totalitarian
experiences, with the intent of distancing themselves from the
past, it does not mean, however, that this was a guarantee of
freedom: in the GDR, East Germany under Soviet control, the use
of the adjective 'democratic' in the official country name (*German
Democratic Republic*) did not prevent its citizens from trying to
flee to the West at every opportunity. In those years, *democracy*
replaced *popular*, to avoid any confusion with those regimes (right
and left) which, while referring to the people, in fact exercised
tight control over the masses. These regimes fostered populism,
vulgarization and annihilation of the real spirit of the people,
simply because these pandered to the worst instincts of the masses
and directed them to the regime's advantage.

Thus, the terms follow the fortunes of politics: if, in the early
twentieth century, there had been a proliferation of *the mass*, often
with significant nods to the left, the second post-war period was
marked by the pursuit of *democracy*, diminished in all its forms.
It could almost be said that democracy in its original and correct
meaning no longer exists. We use this term to indicate something
completely different, which in our minds takes on an old-world
charm and the incommensurability of an ideal. But it is a lost ideal,
its practical implementation is trampled on, betrayed, reshuffled,
invalidated and, at best, taken for granted.

And yet democracy has never been talked about so much. The
subsequent liberalizations which have accompanied the history of
the labour movement in the last century even gave the impression
of an excess of democracy and therefore of the possibility of
restraining its effects to guarantee governability.

But is there really an excess of democracy? It seems to be something of a paradox, since no one seems to be suffering. The widespread feeling is rather that of a disconnection between the citizen and politics, of an incomplete realization of true democratic representation. If, beyond the perfection of the relationship of representation, what we mean is the right of all citizens to be equal in the eyes of the law, the right to enjoy the same social services, freedom of thought, of expression, and movement, then that is something entirely different. In this case one could speak of an 'excess' of democracy, to the point of it being difficult to contain in a society that is no longer homogenized – that is, compressed into patterns of behaviour and collective cohesion.

What does an excess of democracy entail exactly? According to Streeck in his recent *Buying Time*, it is the mortal sin of the overabundance of guarantees on two fronts: on the private front, the high rate of unionization in Western countries is responsible for having pushed up the cost of labour, as well as having introduced a set of regulations for the protection and defence of employment, to the point of pushing capital to move elsewhere.[21] On the public front, there is the debt of the welfare state, accrued due to increasing pressure from public opinion to supply essential goods and services that have enhanced people's quality of life.

The consequences of the combination of these two components have induced an expectation of welfare and social security well above the realistic possibilities which, in the long run, triggered an inverse process at a time when it was no longer possible to maintain that level so high. According to this hypothesis, the excess of democracy is responsible for the financial crisis of 2008, a sort of *redde rationem* ('doomsday') needed to correct an otherwise unstoppable drift that would have led to ruin.

Postdemocracy

Zygmunt Bauman   In Natalie Brafman's article entitled 'Génération Y: du concept marketing à la réalité', published in its 19 May 2013 issue, *Le Monde* pronounced that Generation Y was 'more individualistic and disobedient to bosses, but above all more precarious' – if compared with the 'boom' and 'X' generations that preceded it, that is.

Between themselves, journalists, marketing experts and social researchers (in that order) assembled in the imagined formation (class?, category?) of 'Generation Y' young men and women between about twenty and thirty years of age (that is, born roughly between the middle of the 1980s and the middle of the 1990s). And what is becoming more obvious by the day is that Generation Y, so composed, may have a better-founded claim to the status of a culturally specific 'formation' – that is, a bona fide 'generation' – and so also a better-justified plea for becoming the centre of attention for traders, news-chasers and scholars, than had its predecessors.

It is common to argue that what grounds the claim and justifies the plea is first and foremost the fact that the members of Generation Y are the first humans who have never experienced a world without the internet and know, as well as practise, digital communication 'in real time'. If you share in the widespread assessment of the arrival of informatics as a watershed in human history, you are obliged to view Generation Y as at least a milestone in the history of culture. And it is so viewed – as a milestone; such it is deemed to be, and as such it is recorded. As an appetizer of sorts, Brafman suggests that the curious French habit of pronouncing 'Y', when it is linked to the idea of a generation, in the English way – as 'why' – could be explained by this being a 'questioning generation'. In other words, it is a formation that takes nothing for granted.

Let me add, however, right away, that the questions this generation is in the habit of asking are addressed by and large to the anonymous authors of Wikipedia, to Facebook pals and Twitter addicts – but never to their parents or bosses or 'public authorities', from whom they don't seem to expect relevant, let alone authoritative and reliable, answers that would be worth listening to.

The surfeit of their questions, I guess, is, as in so many other aspects of our consumerist society, an offer-driven demand: with an iPhone as good as grafted onto the body there are constantly, 24 hours a day and 7 days a week, loads of answers feverishly searching for questions as well as throngs of answer-peddlers frantically seeking demand for their services. And I have another suspicion: do the Generation Y people spend so much time on the internet because they are tormented by questions they crave to have answered? Or are the questions which they ask, once connected to the hundreds of their Facebook friends, instead updated versions of Bronisław Malinowski's 'phatic expressions' (such as, for instance, 'How do you do?' or 'How are you?', the kind of elocutions whose only function is to perform a *socializing task*, as opposed to *conveying information*, the task in this case being to announce your presence and availability for socializing – not all that different from the 'small talk' conducted to break boredom, but above all to escape alienation and loneliness, at a crowded party).

When it comes to surfing the infinitely vast internet expanses, the members of Generation Y are indeed unequalled masters. And when it comes to 'being connected', they are the first generation in history to measure the numbers of their friends (translated nowadays primarily as companions-in-connecting) in hundreds, if not thousands. And they are the first to spend most of their awake-time sociating through conversing – though not necessarily aloud, and seldom in full sentences. This is all true. But is it the whole truth about Generation Y? What about that part of the world which they, by definition, did not and could not experience, having therefore had little if any chance to learn how to deal with it face-to-face, without electronic/digital mediation, and what consequences that inescapable encounter might have? That is the part that nonetheless claims, and to a spectacularly formidable and utterly undismissable effect, to determine the rest of – and perhaps even the most important rest of – their lives' truth?

It is that 'rest' which contains the part of the world that supplies another feature which makes Generation Y stand apart from its predecessors: the precariousness of the place they have been offered by a society they are still struggling, with mixed success, to enter. In France, 25 per cent of people below twenty-five years of age remain unemployed. Generation Y as a whole are linked up to the CDD ('Contrat à durée déterminée': fixed-term contract) and *stages* (work experience) – both shrewdly evasive and crudely, mercilessly exploitative expedients. If in 2006 there were about 600,000 *stagiaires* in France, their current number is estimated to vacillate somewhere between 1.2 and 1.5 million. And for most, visiting that liquid-modern purgatory renamed 'training practice' is unavoidable: agreeing and submitting to such expedients as CDD or *stages* is a necessary condition for finally achieving, at the advanced average age of thirty, the possibility of a full-time, 'infinite' duration (?) employment.

An immediate consequence of the frailty and in-built transience of social positions which the so-called 'labour market' is capable of offering is the widely signalled profound change of attitude towards the idea of a 'job' – and particularly of a steady job, a job safe and reliable enough to be capable of determining the medium-term social standing and life prospects of its performer. Generation Y is marked by the unprecedented, and growing, 'job-cynicism' of its members (and no wonder, if for instance, Alexandra de Felice, reputable observer/commentator of the French labour market, expects an average member of Generation Y, if the current trends continue, to change bosses and employers twenty-nine times in the course of their working life – though some other observers, such as Rouen Business School Professor Jean Pralong, call for more realism in estimating the youngsters' chances of matching the pace of job-changing to the cynicism of their job-attitudes: in a labour market in its present condition, it would take a lot of daring and courage to snap one's fingers at the boss and tell him face-to-face that one would rather go than stay with such a pain in the ass).

So, according to Jean Pralong, the youngsters would rather put up with their dreary plight, however off-putting that plight might be, if they were allowed to stay longer in their quasi-jobs. But they seldom are, and if they are they would not know how long the stay of execution could last. One way or another, members of Generation Y differ from their predecessors in a complete, or almost complete, absence of job-related illusions, in a no more than lukewarm commitment (if there is one at all) to the jobs currently held and the companies which offer them, and in a firm conviction that life is elsewhere and a resolution (or at least a desire) to live it elsewhere. This is indeed an attitude that was seldom to be found among the members of the 'boom' and 'X' generations.

Some of the bosses admit that the guilt is on their side. They are reluctant to lay the blame for the resulting disenchantment and nonchalance prevalent among young employees on the youngsters themselves. Brafman quotes Gilles Babinet, a 45-year-old entrepreneur, bewailing the dispossession of the young generation of all, or nearly all, autonomy their fathers had and successfully guarded – priding themselves on possessing the moral, intellectual and economic principles of which their society was presumed to be the guardian and from which it wouldn't allow its members to budge. He believes that the kind of society which Generation Y enters is, on the contrary, anything but seductive: if he were their age, Babinet admits, he'd behave exactly as they do.

As for the youngsters themselves, they are as blunt as their predicament is straightforward: they have not the slightest idea, they say, what tomorrow is likely to bring. The labour market closely guards its secrets – just as impenetrable fortresses do: there is little point in trying to peep inside, let alone attempting to break down the gates. And as for the guessing of its intentions – it's hard to believe that there are any. Tougher and more knowledgeable minds than mine are known mostly for their abominable mis-judgements in the guessing game. In a hazardous world, we have no choice but to be gamblers – whether by choice, or by necessity; and, in the end, it doesn't matter what it is by, does it?

Well, these state-of-the-mind reports are remarkably similar to the confessions of the more thoughtful and sincere among the *precarians* – members of the *precariat*, the most rapidly growing section of our post-credit-collapse and post-certainty world. Pre-carians are defined by having their homes erected (complete with bedrooms and kitchens) on quicksand, and by their own self-confessed ignorance ('no idea what is going to hit me') and impo-tence ('even if I knew, I wouldn't have the power to divert the blow').

It has been thought until now that the appearance and formi-dable, some say explosive, expansion of the precariat, sucking in and incorporating more and more of the former working and middle classes, was a phenomenon arising from the fast-changing *class* structure. It is indeed – but isn't it, in addition, also a matter of a changing *generational* structure, of bringing forth a state of affairs in which the proposition 'Tell me the year of your birth, and I'll tell you which social class you belong to' won't sound so very fanciful at all?

Carlo Bordoni To explain the declining phase of the process of democratization, Colin Crouch introduces the effective concept of 'post-democracy' as a 'crisis of egalitarianism and trivialisation of democratic processes', in which politics loses more and more contact with the citizens and ends up producing an uncomfortable condition that could be defined as 'anti-politics'.[22]

Today we talk about anti-politics in connection with the demonstrations of outrage against corruption, scandals, the squandering of public money and its misappropriation for private interests; against the inefficiency of ethical control reported in the public administration and in the majority of the political parties. The effect of this could only be profound indignation, followed by a move away from politics with a sense of nausea, as well as futility. This is regularly observed in a lower turn-out for elections: however, it is also said that a lower voter turn-out is normal in democratic countries and that it is a positive sign. Yet a move away from politics can only lead to serious consequences that contemporary history has already experienced: anti-politics, equal to the definition of politics as 'something dirty', something not to get involved in, to leave to those who do it professionally and 'sacrifice' themselves for others. It is the direct route towards authoritarianism, already used by Mussolini as a strategy to achieve power.

Moreover, the problem of political representation or delegation has always been debated, often placing democracy and representation in opposition, as irreconcilable terms. Rousseau warned against the easy tendency to delegate popular sovereignty to others out of laziness, to allow people to attend to their own affairs, their family commitments or simply out of disdain: a bad choice that has lethal consequences for personal freedom. Once established, democracy can be circumvented in many ways. It is certainly not a victory that can be achieved easily, given the ease with which it can be called into question.

Among the characterizing effects of postdemocracy, we can list:

(a)   *deregulation*, that is, the cancellation of the rules governing economic relations and the supremacy of finance and stock markets;

(b)   a drop in citizens' participation in political life and elections (although this is often considered to be normal);

(c)   the return of economic liberalism (neoliberalism), entrusting to the private sector part of the functions of the state and management services – which before were 'public' – with the same criteria of economic performance as a private company;

(d) the decline of the welfare state, reserving basic services only for the poorest, i.e. as an exceptional circumstance and not as part of a generalized right for all citizens;

(e) the prevalence of *lobbies*, which increase their power and direct politics in their desired direction;

(f) the show-business of politics, in which advertising techniques are used to produce consensus; the predominance of the figure of the leader that does not lie in the charismatic figure, but relies on the power of the image, market research and a precise communicative project;

(g) a reduction in public investments;

(h) the preservation of the 'formal' aspects of democracy, which at least maintains the appearance of the guarantee of liberty.

Is there any difference between the 'post-democracy' of Crouch and the 'de-democratisation' of Tilly? At first glance, they may seem to be two terms to denote the same concept, i.e. a decrease in democratic guarantees achieved through people fighting long and hard for them. In fact they are two different processes, which can even be combined and cause devastating damage as regards loss of freedom. De-democratization foresees an effective cancellation of certain democratic prerogatives, often for a short period or in order to deal with exceptional events (terrorism, natural disasters). Postdemocracy, on the contrary, is an underhand process, presented as 'natural', which guarantees formal liberties, while demeaning them or emptying them of their real democratic content.

As Tilly observed in the case of India, recovery from 'de-democratisation' is possible – i.e. it is possible to emerge unscathed and regain lost time.[23] It is more difficult to emerge from 'postdemocracy' because it is driven by strong shared interests and has now become part of the culture of our time: the classic example is the introduction of fixed-term employment or contracts, which has formalized job insecurity, with fixed-term contracts portrayed as a necessary practice to meet the demands for greater flexibility on the part of industry.

Wolfgang Streeck suggests that the current financial crisis is a consequence of the failure of democracy, while it is also possible that the current crisis has been induced or guided to re-create social inequality and reduce democracy.[24]

More features converge in this framework, including privatization in the name of progress, profit and efficiency; the removal of
capital from national interests and its 'dematerialization' in the
financial markets; the collapse of the Keynesian model or, more
generally, of government intervention in the economy, and its
replacement with the Hayekian model.[25] A result of this is dimin-
ishing resources: we are relatively poorer now compared to fifty
years ago, but at least we have more technology available and the
means to communicate more easily – this too has its social
consequences.

The struggle between 'capitalism and democracy' is currently
in the phase of the rise of capitalism, at least until the reactions
of the democratic party begin to be felt, aimed at regaining lost
ground in a difficult balancing act.

The fact is that the present condition of democratic *defaillance*
is mainly due to the crisis of the state, to its inability to act
as a strong and decisive interlocutor of social mediation, as
regulator of the economy, as guarantor of security. So much
so – reaffirms Streeck – that the 'private insurance companies
replaced governments and politics as providers of social
security'.[26]

Deregulation, an ambiguous procedure for the removal of
public powers that gives an underlying sense of 'liberation' from
over-restrictive rules, is the first step towards neoliberalism,
privatization of services and the drastic abatement of the welfare
state, which ends with a balanced budget: a contradiction in terms,
because the state is not a public company and is non-profit-
making, but must provide social services and redistribute wealth.
Managing it according to the terms imposed by the EU, which
has convinced its member states to include the practice of a balanced budget in their constitutions, means giving up its primary
prerogatives and fostering the inequality of its citizens. From an
excess of democracy, we pass on, with a sudden jump, to postdemocracy, with the sole purpose of gaining time while waiting for
things to settle down by themselves. The people forget and they
become used to – then resigned to – seeing that privileges are
assured for just a few. This is a formula that, in addition to
weakening the nation-state and stripping it of its powers, works
in the interest of capitalism, which, in carrying out the operation
of *deregulation* and release from the constraints imposed by

the nation-state, finds an unexpected opportunity to grow and consolidate.

As for flexibility at work, the hypothesis is subtly being spread that it has been fostered by the introduction of women into the job market.[27] This is close to saying that female workers have favoured and sought flexibility for their own convenience (as it is compatible with their family needs) and to find new ways of being hired. It follows from this that the female world in search of financial autonomy is responsible for the phenomenon of fixed-term employment contracts, the most shocking result of postdemocracy and the apogee of neoliberalism.

In this extraordinary reversal of reality, in which the result becomes the cause of the facts, we can glimpse a prejudice that was inherent in Fascism, which saw the world as one that was physiologically male and could be guaranteed only by its unity and solidity. It should also be said that women's work has a long consolidated tradition and it certainly did not emerge in the 1990s, when Western countries began to erode the various rights of employment protection that were won in the post-war period and sanctioned by a set of laws generally known as 'the Workers' Statute'. Flexibility in the job market, until then, had been intended to be in favour of the workers, mainly to allow part-time work, flexibility of working hours and the opportunity to move. The statistical data on the extent of women's work in Europe and the US show the presence of women, especially in public employment, without it serving to justify a reduction in union guarantees.

As the neoliberal idea regains strength, bringing more benefit to capital, making it more profitable, the option of flexibility extends to employers, introducing the possibility of fixed-term or short-term contracts, necessary to meet the temporary needs of production and therefore exempted from union rules and the inflexibility of employment contracts. Deviously presented as an unusual and exceptional scheme, aimed at promoting employment and providing new opportunities for young people and women, it has been welcomed and supported by the media and also by the left-wing parties, who have not grasped its negative potential to upset the labour market and reinvigorate capitalism, after a long period of obfuscation.

As for the de-materialization of capital, it is a phenomenon to be considered carefully in its extraordinary ability to innovate radically in the economy: an unforeseen change that no previous theory had considered, and no theory could have prevented its serious social consequences.

In the traditional economy, capital has a concrete and visible form. It is integrated in land, buildings, factories and machines for manufacture. Therefore, it has a weight and a territorial permanence: in the industrial revolution, the presence of capital was symbolized by the chimney stacks that filled the sky with smoke in the mining areas; in the nineteenth century, by the working masses who came out of the factories at the end of their shift; in the twentieth century, by the skyscrapers of the great American *holding companies*. The factory is a physical place in which that continuity of interests and existential conditions that favours the formation of class-consciousness is established.

However, the de-materialization of capital – that is, its transformation (or liquefaction) into financial products which, given their nature, can be transferred from one point of the globe to another and invested in diversified assets – breaks with this tradition and enables its emancipation from politics. It frees capital from the constraints of the social tradition that the state had managed to impose on it. This 'liquefaction' of capital, which has its inevitable counterpart in the liquid society,[28] severely limits the possibility of state intervention in the economy, which in the first half of the twentieth century, and particularly after the grave crisis of 1929, had represented the dream of a resolute alliance between capitalism and democracy.

Among the reasons for the liquefaction of capital we can find the de-materialization of labour, i.e. the gradual decommissioning of heavy industry; the postindustrialization of the third industrial revolution, which has made the great factories that employed huge amounts of manpower obsolete; the exponential growth of services, automation of production processes; miniaturization and the new technologies.

This process, which began in the 1970s and developed over the next thirty years, has freed capital from its contingent commitment, has released it from long-term investments and has, so to speak, deprived it of any definite purpose. So, it could be said, and not without a certain degree of irony, that capital – in the process of de-industrialization – was the first 'insecure element' of the new economic phase.

It is forced to seek, from time to time, new investment opportunities, always ready to change face, substance, location – often purely virtual – at the risk of evaporating in the blinking of an eye, because of poor choices or bad timing. But it is strong enough, more than ever, to seize the best opportunities and exploit them to its advantage, while respecting the principles of free competition and a revived *laissez-faire* without boundaries that no nation-state is able to oppose.

The crux is still social control: when a community, a group or a population spirals out of control, it always generates a counter-reaction. It is a reflection that has nothing spontaneous about it, but responds to specific political needs for order and balance. What might have been admissible and therefore granted, guaranteed, allowed in a mass society, is no longer feasible in a de-massified society.

The perfect balance of totalitarianism lay in granting certain privileges in exchange for freedom; that of mass society on some formal liberties in exchange for consumerism and conformity. Social *liquefaction* actually appears with an uncontrolled spread, which, in the eyes of the system, is no longer comprehensible and is unstoppable. Over time, the system has lost most of its effective tools for exercising control, either directly (authoritarianism, dictatorship) or indirectly (single-mindedness, consumerism, monopoly on communications, fobbing off the masses through media spiel): it cannot even employ the comforting support of ideologies to maintain the aggregation of social groups, on a totally uncritical basis, relying on emotional and irrational persuasion.

To regain control and restore the order that has been altered, it is necessary to impose a revision of the rules. It would be impossible to do so by force (an anti-historical choice), let alone by relying on media consensus.

The instrument most suited to our times can only be the economy. It certainly has the potential to work in a liquid world: it goes beyond the understanding of most people; it is so complex as to be difficult even for insiders; it is transient, mobile and easily influenced. It is not subject to democracy, because it is not possible to resort to universal suffrage to direct it. It has its own rules and definite consequences. The only unequivocal certainty of a liquefied and insecure world. The economic manoeuvres have immediate repercussions for democracy; they manage to establish equality or inequality among men more than laws and revolutions.

What is the use of everyone being equal on paper, having the same opportunities, and freedom of action and thought, if it just takes a few economic restrictions to call everything into question?

Bringing back social differences, restoring priorities, allows the system to acquire and maintain social control. Pauperizing means dividing and controlling. Just put the weaker sections of the population in the position of not having access to the same benefits as before, exclude them from opportunities, separate them from the more fortunate. In fact, deprive them of freedom, even if freedom and democracy are proclaimed and exalted at every opportunity. The victims of the economic crisis are isolated, fearful, depressed and alone in facing an uncertain future.

Impermanence and instability are reflected in every aspect of daily life, from work to romantic relationships, which even influences architecture and the manufacturing industry (we build houses that have a limited life span; products of the hyper-tech industry are inevitably outmoded quickly), in a more and more frenetic race against time. Liquid society is a fast-flowing society that grinds and erodes everything increasingly rapidly and, for this reason, it exists in a state of continuous evolution: the state of transition is its state of stability.

For a new global order

Carlo Bordoni Democracy is a mobile, fluctuating concept, which is destined to evolve along with society. Just think of the transformation it underwent at the time of Tocqueville: from government of the people, feared for its illiberal implications (the dictatorship of the majority), it has acquired a much broader social sense, meaning – on the basis of the American experience – the general aspiration towards equality and the same rights for all.

It is obvious that since then, since the first half of the nineteenth century, the idea of democracy could not have remained the same without suffering repercussions from a society that was changing so rapidly. We had to expect an escalation of protests at street level, where the conditions of life are more stressful: because it is the economy, as always, that instigates revolt, but behind it there is always a real need for change, which the protagonists themselves are often not aware of.

The protests in Egypt, Turkey and Brazil suggest a worsening of the crisis of democracy, in which citizens play a major role. They are much more attentive, more vigilant than the traditional passive masses who became disinterested in politics after electing their leader. We can speak no longer of masses but of multitudes, and it is not simply a question of a semantic difference. The new social differences are necessary to restore those margins of power that democratization has eroded, enabling the process of individual self-awareness to develop online. Self-awareness is equivalent to the liberation of our own impulses and so to revolution against order, to a refusal to accept rules imposed from the outside. For this reason, any constituted authority, from the earliest examples in communities and in modern society itself, is intended first and foremost to implement social control. When he considers the innovative spontaneous movements that were created on the internet, such as *Occupy Wall Street*, the *Indignados* and the *Arab Spring*, Manuel Castells forgets that they are nothing more than the natural consequence of a slackening of social control, examples of which are repeated throughout history, each time with different characteristics and modalities, when the authority of institutions and governments starts to experience crisis.[29] However, these movements are not the cause but the direct, socially significant consequence of that crisis. A tangible sign that the system is no longer able to take the strain and new social balances need to be found – whether they are produced by revolutions, reforms or new elections has little importance.

Governance at the supranational level, in the face of the demassification process, regains control of the individual by using the economic crisis and promoting new social differences. The long and painful path to democratization and to the elimination of social inequality, which began in the nineteenth century, involved a radical revision process, almost a *restoration* through the economy. Today, the economy is the most effective instrument of social control, as were consumerism in the 1960s and 1980s, totalitarianism in the 1930s and forced urbanization in the eighteenth century.

But if we allow the economy and the markets to steer our lives, we will find ourselves in a globalized society that has marked social differences, composed of an impoverished majority that is deprived of guarantees and services and crushed down into a sort of equality, alongside a privileged minority: privileged not only because of their high income, but also because they enjoy certain concessions and the opportunity to access all kinds of benefits.

A deep social division, far more radical than the traditional opposition between mass and *elite*, will re-present an *overclass* – as suggested by Richard Rorty in the epigraph above – but in a more exasperating and generalized form.

And what of the others? Those who live an average life?

De-massified society has reached a perfect level of equality: a society of impoverished individuals who are gratified by the high-tech industry and the great ease of interpersonal communication, but who are incapable of self-regulated politics because it is removed from their control.

Distanced, deferred, dematerialized, incomprehensible: these are the features of the new politics – directed essentially by economic decisions – completely removed from the citizens and implicitly delegated to the *top-level government executives* of global power that have no face. The ordinary citizen can only have responsibility for local-level politics, which has no significant sphere of action, and is limited to the management of routine matters – almost like a condominium meeting, in which the costs of ordinary and extraordinary maintenance are managed, and comfort can be found in the eternal game of representation.

In a de-massified society, we no longer speak of *real* representation. What need is there of representation at the highest level (given that the ordinary citizen does not understand the complexity of economic issues on a global level and is not competent to make decisions), when democracy – i.e. real democracy, the one that really concerns people – is fully realized in everyday issues? Is government of the people not democracy? And the people are reassured by the perfect government of local autonomy, of choices and resources that concern them.

The question of a separation between power and politics will thus be resolved *democratically*: power and politics united at a local level, but aimed at a global level, whose jurisdiction is reserved to a power (economic) without politics. Furthermore, we cannot speak of the existence of a *global citizen*, but only of a local citizen who is affected by globalization. Who can say that this is not progress? Everyone is equal in the eyes of the great laws of economics, of the inscrutable movements of the economic markets. All are deprived of obsolete social guarantees; all precarious, insecure and impoverished.

People are freed from the obsession with consumerism, from the oppression of the single mind, from mass culture; free to think, express opinions, communicate and participate; freed from strain and from labour. Crisis has this immense liberating power. But democracy is something else.

Zygmunt Bauman I am not prepared, I am afraid, to visualize (let alone to draw a blueprint of) a 'new global order'. As Reinhart Koselleck, whom I quoted before, insisted, it would be utterly irresponsible to do so when we are climbing, as now, a steep slope and still far from the mountain pass that will (we can only hope) open to a view of the other side of the mountain crest. The most I can dare is to think of the impassable obstacles on the way to the top: things we will have to jump over or shift out of the way if we wish the mountain pass through to a new order ever to be reached. Some of these obstacles were listed at the beginning of our conversation, and so there is no need to name them once more. Allow me therefore to add one to the list: in my view, one of the most forbidable obstacles, and the least easy to negotiate, yet one which most effectively bars our ascent and our chance of ever reaching the pass – though it has been unduly omitted so far from our discussion. What I have in mind is what I called elsewhere (in *Consuming Life*) the 'consumerist syndrome'.[30]

Consumerist syndrome posits the totality of the inhabited world – complete with its inanimate and animate, animal as well as human, occupants – as a huge container filled to the brim with nothing else but objects of potential consumption. It thereby justifies and promotes the perception, assessment and evaluation of each and every worldly entity according to the standards set in the practices of consumer markets. Those standards establish starkly a-symmetrical relations between clients and commodities, consumers and consumer goods: the former expecting from the latter solely the gratification of their needs, desires and wants, while the latter derive their sole meaning and value from the

degree to which they meet those expectations. Consumers are free
to set apart the desirable from the un-desirable or indifferent
objects – as well as free to determine to what extent the objects
deemed desirable met their expectations and for how long those
objects retained their assumed desirability unimpaired.

To put it in a nutshell: it is the consumers' desires, and only
those, that count, first and last. It is only in the commercials (as
in the memorable TV advertisement depicting marching columns
of fungi shouting 'Make room for the Mushrooms!') that the
objects of desire share in their consumers' pleasures or suffer
pangs of conscience when they frustrate the consumers' expectations. No one really believes that the objects of consumption,
archetypal 'things' devoid of senses, thoughts and emotions of
their own, would resent rejection or termination of their services
(indeed, being consigned to a rubbish tip). However satisfying the
consuming sensations might have been, their beneficiaries owe
nothing in exchange to the sources of their pleasures. Most certainly, they don't need to swear indefinite loyalty to the objects of
consumption. The 'things' meant for consumption retain their
utility for consumers – their one and only *raison d'être* – only as
long as their estimated pleasure-giving capacity remains undimin-
ished (and not for a moment longer).

Once that object's pleasure-generating capacity falls below the
postulated or endurable/acceptable level, the time is ripe to get rid
of the bland and bleak thing – that unexciting, pale replica or
rather ugly caricature of the object that once glittered/tempted its
way into being desired. The cause of its degradation and disposal
is not necessarily an unwelcome change (or any change for that
matter) that took place in the object itself; it could instead be – and
all too often is – something that happened to the contents of the
gallery where the prospective objects of desire are displayed,
sought, viewed, appreciated and appropriated: a previously absent
or overlooked object that is somehow better equipped to lavish
pleasurable sensations, and so more promising and tempting than
the one already possessed and used, has now been spotted in the
shop window or on the shop shelf. Or perhaps using/enjoying the
current object of desire went on for long enough to prompt a sort
of 'satisfaction fatigue', particularly because its potential replacements have not yet been tried and so augur novel, heretofore un-
experienced, unknown and untried delights, which are believed

for that reason alone to be superior and therefore endowed (for the moment, at least) with more seductive power. Whatever the reason, it gets more and more difficult – nay, impossible – to imagine why the thing that has lost much or all of its capacity to entertain should not be duly sent off to where it now belongs – to the rubbish dump.

What, however, if the 'thing' in question happens to be another sentient and conscious, feeling, thinking, judging and choosing entity: in short, another human being? However bizarre this may be, this question is anything but fanciful. Quite a while ago, Anthony Giddens, one of the most influential sociologists of recent decades, announced the advent of 'pure relations' – that is, relations with no commitments of undefined length and reach. 'Pure relations' are founded on nothing else except the gratification drawn from them – and once that gratification dwindles and fades, or is dwarfed by the availability of a gratification even more profound, there is no reason whatsoever for them to be continued. Please note, however, that 'being gratified' is in this case a *two-pronged* affair. To assemble a 'pure relation', *both* partners need to expect from it gratification of their desires. To dis-assemble it, however, the disgruntlement and disaffection of *one* partner suffices. Putting the relationship together calls for a *bilateral* decision – taking it apart can be done *unilaterally*.

Each of the two partners in a pure relationship, in turn or simultaneously, attempts to play the subject to the other's object. Each one, in turn or simultaneously, may, however, come across an object that stoutly refuses to accept the role of a 'thing' while attempting instead to degrade her/his protagonist to the 'thingy' status and thereby foiling his/her pretensions and aspirations to the status of 'subject'. There is a paradox, therefore, of an unresolvable sort: each partner enters a 'pure relationship' assuming his/her own right to subjectivity and the counterpart's demotion/submission to the status of thing; however, any partner's success in making that assumption come true (that is, effectively disarming the other of his/her right to subjectivity) portends the end to the relationship.

A 'pure relationship' is therefore based on fiction and wouldn't survive the revelation of its truth: of the essential un-transferability of the subject/object division endemic to the consumerist pattern to the realm of inter-human relationships. Rejection may arrive at any moment, with little or no notice; bonds are not really binding, they are endemically unstable and unreliable – just one more unknown and anxiety-generating variable in the insoluble equation called 'life'. As long as their relation stays 'pure', with an anchor cast in no other haven than that of desire-gratification, both partners are doomed to the agony of possible rejection or condemned to a bitter awakening from their illusions. That awakening is bound to be all the more bitter because the paradox lurking at the heart of the 'purity' has not been recognized by them in advance, and therefore not enough – or nothing – has been done by them to negotiate a satisfactory, or at least bearable, compromise between irreconcilable statuses.

The advent and prevalence of 'pure relations' have been widely yet wrongly interpreted as a huge step on the road to 'liberation' of the individual (the latter having been, willy-nilly, reinterpreted as being free from constraints which all obligations to others are bound to set on one's own choices). What makes this interpretation questionable is, however, that the notion of 'mutuality' is, in this case, a gross, and unfounded, exaggeration. The coincidence of both parties in a relationship being simultaneously satisfied does not necessarily create mutuality: after all, it means no more than that each of the individuals in the relationship is satisfied *at the same time* – but what stops the relationship short of genuine mutuality is its inbuilt – sometimes consoling, but other times haunting and harrowing – expectation: also a not-to-be-played-down constraint on individual freedom. The essential distinction of 'networks' – the name selected these days to replace the old-fashioned, and putatively outdated, ideas of 'community' or 'communion' – is precisely this right to *unilateral* termination. Unlike communities, networks are individually put together and individually re-shuffled or dismantled, and, for their persistence, can rely on the individual will as their sole, however volatile, foundation. In a relationship, however, *two* individuals meet. A morally 'insensitivized' individual (that is, one who has been enabled and is willing to take no account of the welfare of another) is willy-nilly situated simultaneously at the receiving end of the moral insensitivity of the objects of his/her own moral insensitivity. 'Pure relations' augur not so much mutuality of liberation, as mutuality of moral insensitivity. The Levinasian 'party of two' stops being a seedbed of morality. It turns instead into a factor of *adiaphorization* (that is, exemption from the realm of moral evaluation) of the specifically *liquid*-modern variety, complementing – while also, all too often, supplanting – the *solid*-modern, bureaucratic variety.

What is being done to things is naturally, in any place or time, assumed to be 'adiaphoric' – neither good nor bad, neither recommended nor condemned. Didn't God give Adam unquestionable rule over them, including the power to name them, which means defining them? The liquid-modern variety of adiaphorization is cut after the pattern of consumer–commodity relations, and its effectiveness relies on the transplantation of that pattern into interhuman relations. As consumers, we do not swear interminable loyalty to the commodity we seek and purchase in order to satisfy our needs or desires, and continue to use its services as long as it delivers on our expectation, but no longer – or until we come across another commodity that promises to gratify the same desires more thoroughly than the one we purchased before. All consumer goods, including those somewhat hypocritically and deceitfully described as 'durable', are eminently exchangeable and expendable; in a consumerist – that is, consumption-inspired and consumption-servicing – culture, the time distance between purchase and disposal tends to shrink fast. Finally, the delights derived from the objects of consumption shift from their use to their appropriation. The longevity of use tends to be shortened and the incidents of rejection and disposal tend to become ever more frequent as the objects' capacity to satisfy (and thus to remain desired) tends to be used up faster. While the consumerist attitude may lubricate the wheels of the *economy*, it sprinkles sand into the bearings of *morality*.

This is not, though, the sole calamity that affects morally saturated actions in a liquid-modern setting. As calculation of gains can never fully subdue and stifle the tacit, yet admittedly refractory and stubbornly insubordinate, pressures of the moral impulse, neglect of moral commands and disregarding of the responsibility evoked – in Levinas' terms, by the 'Face of an-Other' – leaves behind a bitter aftertaste, known by the name of 'pangs of conscience' or 'moral scruples'. Here again, consumerist offers come to the rescue: the sin of moral negligence can be repented and absolved with shop-supplied gifts, as the act of shopping – however selfish and self-referential its true motives and the temptations that made it happen might be – is re-presented as a moral deed.

Capitalizing on redemptive moral urges instigated by the misde-
meanour it generated itself, and which it has encouraged and
intensified, consumerist culture thereby transforms every shop and
service agency into a pharmacy purveying tranquillizers and anaes-
thetic drugs: in this case, the drugs meant to mitigate, or placate
altogether, *moral*, instead of physical, pains. As the moral negligence grows in its reach and intensity, the demand for painkillers
rises unstoppably, and consumption of moral tranquillizers turns
into addiction. As a result, induced/contrived moral insensitivity
tends to turn into a compulsion or a 'second nature': into a permanent and quasi-universal condition – with moral pains being
divested in consequence of their salutary warning/alerting/activat-
ing role. With moral pains smothered before they turn truly vexing
and worrying, the web of human bonds woven out of moral yarn
becomes increasingly frail and fragile, falling apart at the seams.
With citizens trained to search for salvation from their troubles
and solution of their problems in consumer markets, politics may
(or is prompted, pushed and ultimately coerced to) interpellate its
subjects as consumers first and citizens a distant second; and rede-
fine consumer zeal as a citizen's virtue, and consumer activity as
fulfilment of a citizen's primary duty.

Not just the politics and survival of community are threatened.
Our person-to-person togetherness, and the satisfaction, the fulfilment, we draw from it, also face danger when confronted with
the combined pressure of a consumerist world-view and the ideal
of 'pure relations'. 'The ultimate goal of technology, the telos of
techne', suggested Jonathan Franzen in the commencement speech
delivered on 21 May 2011 at Kenyon College, 'is to replace a
natural world that's indifferent to our wishes – a world of hurri-
canes and hardships and breakable hearts, a world of resistance
– with a world so responsive to our wishes as to be, effectively, a
mere extension of the self.' It is all about convenience, stupid –
about an effortless comfort and comfortable effortlessness;
about making the world obedient and pliable; about excising from
the world all that would stand, obstinately and pugnaciously,
between will and reality. Correction: as reality is what resists the
will, it is all about getting rid of reality. It is about living in the
world made of one's wishes alone; of mine and your wishes, of
our – the purchasers, consumers, users and beneficiaries of technology – wishes.

Notes

1 R. Rorty, *Philosophy and Social Hope*, Penguin, 1999, p. 233.
2 M. Horkheimer and T. W. Adorno, *Dialectic of Enlightenment* (1947), trans. J. Cumming, Verso, 1997.
3 J.-P. Sartre, *The Imaginary: A Phenomenological Psychology of the Imagination* (1940), trans. J. Webber, Routledge, 2004.
4 T. Lucretius Caro, *The Nature of Things*, Book V, ed. R. Jenkyns, Penguin, 2007:

> Usus et impigrae simul experientia mentis
> paulatim docuit pedetemptim progredientis.
> sic unum quicquid paulatim protrahit aetas
> in medium ratioque in luminis erigit oras
> (By practice and the mind's experience,
> As men walked forward step by eager step.
> Thus time draws forward each and everything
> Little by little into the midst of men,
> And reason uplifts it to the shores of light).

5 J. B. Bury, *The Idea of Progress: An Inquiry into its Origin and Growth* (1920), McMillan, 1932, pp. 6–7: 'The idea of human Progress then is a theory which involves a synthesis of the past and a prophecy of the future. It is based on an interpretation of history which regards men as slowly advancing . . . in a definite and desirable direction, and infers that this progress will continue indefinitely. And it implies that, as *The issue of the earth's great business*, a condition of general happiness will ultimately be enjoyed, which will justify the whole process of civilisation.'
6 A. Gorz, *Critique of Economic Reason* (1988), Verso, 2011.
7 G. Lipovetsky, *Le bonheur paradoxal: essai sur la société d'hyperconsommation*, Gallimard, 2006.
8 S. Latouche, *Farewell to Growth* (2007), trans. D. Macey, Polity, 2009.
9 E. Morin, *La Voie: pour l'avenir de l'humanité*, Fayard, 2011.
10 J. Gray, *The Silence of Animals: On Progress and Other Modern Myths*, Penguin, 2013, pp. 6–7.
11 See H. Welzer, *Climate Wars: Why People Will Be Killed in the Twenty-first Century*, trans. P. Camiller, Polity, 2012, p. 176.
12 S. P. Huntington, *The Clash of Civilizations and the Remaking of World Order*, Free Press, 2002
13 J. L. Fischer, *Krize demokracie. I. Svoboda, II. Řád* (1933), Karolinum, 2005.

14 L. Canfora, *Democracy in Europe: A History of an Ideology*, trans. S. Jones, Wiley-Blackwell, 2006.

15 J.-J. Rousseau, *The Social Contract* (1762), Oxford, 2008, p. 101.

16 Ibid., p. 127.

17 A. de Tocqueville, *Democracy in America* (1835–40), Penguin, 2003. But the idea of freeing democracy from the concept of a numerical majority is already present in Aristotle: see Canfora, *Democracy in Europe*, pp. 249–50.

18 B. Moore Jr, *Social Origins of Dictatorship and Democracy: Lord and Peasant in the Making of the Modern World* (1966), Beacon Press, 1967, p. 418.

19 C. Tilly, *Democracy*, Cambridge University Press, 2007.

20 Canfora, *Democracy in Europe*, p. 250.

21 W. Streeck, *Buying Time: The Delayed Crisis of Democratic Capitalism*, trans. P. Camiller, Verso, 2014.

22 C. Crouch, *Post-democracy*, Polity, 2004.

23 Tilly, *Democracy*, p. 81.

24 Streeck, *Buying Time*, p. 48.

25 F. A. Von Hayek is the author of a well-established liberal theory that has met with considerable success: see *Law, Legislation and Liberty: A New Statement of the Liberal Principles of Justice and Political Economy* (1973–9), Routledge, 2012.

26 Streeck, *Buying Time*, p. 45.

27 Ibid., p. 17.

28 But while the liquid society produces uncertainty and instability in individuals, the liquefaction of capital, on the contrary, is a source of certainty, from the moment that the flexibility of financial resources can find productive investments with greater rapidity in other parts of the world.

29 M. Castells, *Networks of Outrage and Hope*, Polity, 2012.

30 Z. Bauman, *Consuming Life*, Polity, 2007.

Index

consumerism, 10, 16, 52, 75, 91, 119, 120–1, 145, 147
consumerist syndrome, 149–54
crises
  2008. *See* crisis (2008-)
  crises of transition, 68, 89–90
  definition, 1–12
  economic crises, 1–2, 3, 4, 6, 7–8
  etymology, 1
  modernity, 55–110
  oil crisis (1970s), 90
  state, 1–52, 115–16
crisis (2008-)
  characteristics, 3
  crisis of agency, 10, 22, 24, 95, 103, 124
  duration, 6–7, 12, 59
  excess of democracy, 135
  failure of democracy, 141–2
  financial crisis, 4–6
  international cooperation and, 21
  origins, 3–4
  power–politics divorce, 12–26, 29–32, 71, 94–5, 148–9
  social and economic transformation, 59
critical theory, 78
Crouch, Colin, 139–40, 141
cultural revolution, 91, 114, 124
culture, economy and, 113–14
Cyprus, 38
Czech Republic, 96, 97–8, 101–2

D'Azeglio, Massimo, 26
Decadentism, 90
deconstruction, 57, 84, 87–8
deflationary politics, 6
demagogues, 66–7, 132
demassification, 16, 40, 42–3, 71, 90, 92, 145, 147–8

dematerialization of capital, 142, 143–4
democracy
  ancient Greece, 128–9
  capitalism and, 142
  choices, 23
  crisis, 113–54
  de-democratization, 133, 141
  elections, 19–20, 140
  etymology, 128–9
  excess of democracy, 135, 142
  false democracy, 15, 58
  formal aspects, 141
  meanings, 128, 130–1, 134
  neoliberalism and, 33
  new global order, 146–54
  participation, 14, 31, 55, 114, 134, 140, 149
  political leaders, 97–8, 100–2, 141
  postdemocracy, 135–46
  power–politics divorce, 12–26, 29–32, 71, 94–5, 148–9
  progress and, 113–28
  representation, 21, 40, 41, 43, 124, 132–3, 140, 148
  Rousseau, 129–30
Democritus, 118
deregulation, 10, 17, 20–1, 100, 140, 142–3
Derrida, Jacques, 87–8, 91
Descartes, René, 34, 118
Destutt de Tracy, Antoine-Louis-Claude, 71
Dio Cassius Cocceianus, 128
disasters, 55–6, 63
Drucker, Peter, 9

liquid society, 16, 28, 50–1, 61,
  78, 86–9, 93, 93–4, 137,
  144–6, 153
Lisbon earthquake (1755), 55–6,
  63
lobbies, 15, 29, 141
local government, 116–17
Lucretius, Titus Carus, 118
Luddites, 69
Luther, Martin, 70
Lyotard, Jean-François, 55, 71,
  85, 89, 90, 91, 94

Machiavelli, Niccolò, 36
McLuhan, Marshall, 30, 105
Malinowski, Bronislaw, 137
Mao Zedung, 91
markets
  financial markets, 4, 115, 117,
    140, 142, 143–5
  God and, 25–6
  invisible hand, 10–11
  labour markets, 92–3, 137–9,
    143, 144–5
  neoliberalism, 17
  non-places, 31, 115
  statism without state, 15, 29
Marx, Karl, 24, 92, 113, 119
Marxism, 88, 104–5, 131
mass culture, 43, 77, 149
mass society, 16, 92, 94, 145
Mayakowski, Vladimir, 84
media
  fobbing off the masses, 145
  political leaders and, 141
  power and, 42
  subjectivism and, 81
  See also social media
Merkel, Angela, 36–7, 38
Mersenne, Marin, 34
Merton, Robert K., 109–10
Mies van der Rohe, Ludwig, 77
migration, 13, 125–6

modernity
  advent, 68–9
  architecture, 77
  consumerism, 120–1
  crisis, 55–110
  deconstruction and denial,
    87–104
  dissolution, 26, 67–76
  end of history, 104–10
  end of postmodernity, 76–87
  foundations, 108, 118
  good society models, 60
  illusions, 60–1
  liquid modernity, 16, 28, 50–1,
    61, 78, 86–9, 93, 93–4, 137,
    144–6, 153
  mass society, 16, 92
  meaning, 69
  promises withdrawn, 55–67
  state and private industry, 116
  symbols, 67, 73
  work ethic, 117–22
Montesquieu, Charles de, 118
Moore, Barrington, jr, 132
moral catastrophes, 55
Morin, Edgar, 121–2, 130
Moro, Aldo, 91
Moses, 35
Mubarak, Hosni, 96
multinational companies, 4, 29,
  71, 125
Münster, Treaty of (1648), 27–8,
  33
Mussolini, Benito, 140
Myspace, 96

nation
  crisis, 27
  cultural identity, 27, 42
  meaning, 26
  state and nation, 26–39
nation-state. *See* state
nationalism, 14–15, 47